Did Jesus Descend into Hell?

Biblical Insights into a Curious Proposition

By
Steven A. Carlson

Copyright © 2022, Steven A. Carlson
All Rights Reserved
ISBN: 978-0-9827915-9-2
Printed in the United States of America

This edition published in March 2022 in association with

Guardian Publishing, LLC
Holt, Michigan

guardianpublishingllc.com

Other Books Available from Guardian Publishing, LLC:

Baptism and the Battle for Souls – *Faith that Demands Obedience*
Baptism and the Plan of Salvation – *Restoring the New Testament Gospel*
Pentecost – *The Sanctioning of the Apostles*
One Bible…And Yet, So Many Beliefs – *Exploring the Doctrinal Chaos*
Christian Principles: Raising the Bar – *Engaging Lessons from the Sermon on the Mount*
Born of Water and the Spirit – *Entering the Kingdom*
Good News for Everyone! – *Life-Changing Encounters in the Gospel of John*
Saved by Grace *(Ephesians 2: 8-9)*…**Judged According to Works** *(Revelation 20: 12)*

All rights reserved. No part of this publication may be reproduced, stored in a retrieval system, or transmitted in any form or by any means – electronic, mechanical, photocopying, recording, or any other – except for brief quotations in printed reviews, without the prior written permission of the publisher.

All Scripture quotations, unless otherwise noted, are taken from the Holy Bible: New American Standard Version (NASV), Copyright © 2002. Used by permission of the Zondervan Corporation, all rights reserved.

Table of Contents

TITLE	PAGE
PREFACE	1

-- SECTION 1: LIFE, DEATH, AND GOD'S WORD --

CHAPTER 1: WHAT SCRIPTURE REVEALS ABOUT DEATH 6
- INTRODUCTION OF DEATH 6
- DEATH IN THE OLD TESTAMENT 8
- DEATH IN THE NEW TESTAMENT 9
- THE UNSEEN WORLD 9

CHAPTER 2: WHAT SCRIPTURE REVEALS ABOUT SPIRITUAL DOMAINS 11
- HEAVEN 11
- PARADISE 12
- SHE'OL/HÁDES 13
- TARTARUS 14
- HELL 16
- THE UNKNOWABLE 18

CHAPTER 3: WHAT SCRIPTURE REVEALS ABOUT SOUL AND SPIRIT 20
- CREATION 20
- SOUL 22
- SPIRIT 24
- DICHOTOMY VS TRICHOTOMY 29

CHAPTER 4: WHAT SCRIPTURE REVEALS ABOUT RESURRECTION 32
- PERISHABLE VS IMPERISHABLE 32
- TYPES OF RESURRECTION 33

CHAPTER 5: DIFFICULT BIBLE PASSAGES 37
- APPROACHING SCRIPTURE 37
- DIFFICULT BIBLICAL PASSAGES 39
- HANDLING DIFFICULT PASSAGES 40

-- SECTION 2: PROCLAMATION TO SPIRITS IN PRISON --

CHAPTER 6: ALIVE IN THE SPIRIT - 1 PETER 3: 18 44
- A CONTROVERSIAL TEXT 44
- CONTEXT 45
- PUT TO DEATH IN THE FLESH 46
- MADE ALIVE IN THE SPIRIT 47

TITLE	PAGE
CHAPTER 7: GOING AND PROCLAIMING - 1 PETER 3: 19-20	*53*
IN WHICH	53
HAVING GONE	55
THE SPIRITS	57
THE PRISON	63
THE PROCLAMATION	65
CHAPTER 8: BAPTISM AND ASCENSION - 1 PETER 3: 21-22	*69*
CORRESPONDING TO THAT	69
BAPTISM SAVES	70
AN APPEAL	71
THROUGH THE RESURRECTION	72
ASCENDED	72
CHAPTER 9: FAITHFUL IN JUDGMENT - 1 PETER 4: 1-6	*74*
CHANGED LIFE	74
THE PAST IS THE PAST	75
JUDGMENT	76
PREACHING THE GOSPEL	76

-- SECTION 3: SURVEYING THE BIBLICAL LANDSCAPE --

CHAPTER 10: PERUSING SCRIPTURE	*82*
ADDRESSING GOD'S WORD	82
THE OLD TESTAMENT	83
THE NEW TESTAMENT	83
CHAPTER 11: PSALM 16: 10-11	*85*
YOUR HOLY ONE	85
NOT ABANDONED TO SHE'OL	86
CHAPTER 12: PSALM 71: 20	*88*
REVIVAL	88
CHAPTER 13: PSALM 88: 10-12	*90*
WONDERS FOR THE DEAD	90
AT DEATH'S DOOR	91
CHAPTER 14: EZEKIEL 26: 20	*93*
DOWN TO THE PIT…LOWER PARTS OF THE EARTH	93
COMPARISON TO ANTEDILUVIANS	94
CHAPTER 15: HOSEA 13: 14	*96*
REDEMPTION FROM DEATH	96
CHAPTER 16: MATTHEW 12: 38-40	*98*
THE SIGN OF JONAH	98
HEART OF THE EARTH	99
CHAPTER 17: ACTS 2: 24-35	*101*
THE AGONY OF DEATH	101
THE JUXTAPOSITION	102

TITLE	PAGE
CHAPTER 18: ROMANS 10: 6-7	*104*
THE ABYSS	104
THE JEWISH PERSPECTIVE	105
CHAPTER 19: EPHESIANS 4: 7-14	*106*
GRACE	106
HE ASCENDED	107
HE DESCENDED	108
CHAPTER 20: REVELATION 1: 17-18	*111*
THE KEYS OF DEATH AND OF HÁDES	111
A BATTLE FOR THE KEYS	112
POWER OF DEATH	112
CHAPTER 21: HELL, HÁDES, & PARADISE	*116*
HELL AND HÁDES	116
PARADISE IN HÁDES	118
THE PARADISEAN THEORY	118
CHAPTER 22: PEERING BEHIND THE STONE	*122*
REASONED INFERENCE	122
HÁDES VS. HELL	122
JESUS IN HÁDES	124
JESUS WENT TO PARADISE	125
JESUS IN PARADISE	126
CONCLUSION	127
BIBLIOGRAPHY	*129*

Preface

In the world of Christendom, a multitude of views have been advanced concerning the design of the spiritual world and exactly what awaits an individual who passes from this physical life. Among the more interesting doctrinal stances about that world is the claim that, after his crucifixion and while his physical body lay lifeless in the tomb, Jesus' spirit traveled to the spiritual domain known as Hell[1] – a journey often referred to as *The Descensus*. There, it is said, he preached the gospel message he had delivered to the Jews during his days on earth. Many who share this belief also teach that he did this to offer salvation to those who, prior to the introduction of the covenant of grace, had been unfaithful to God.

This is, of course, an oversimplification of the doctrine in question. Numerous shades of this teaching exist with some claiming that Jesus' spirit traveled to the fiery Hell during his time in the tomb while others insist that he went to a waiting place known as Hádes. Some believe he preached the gospel to those in Hell while others teach that he simply went there to proclaim victory over sin and death. What one believes about the days between Jesus' death and resurrection depends, in large part, on that individual's approach to certain passages of Scripture from which this doctrine has been derived.

When and where did these beliefs concerning Jesus' days in the tomb originate? The teaching came down through the Roman Catholic Church and can be found in what is known as The Apostles' Creed, which is intended as a synopsis of apostolic doctrine. In its original spoken form, the creed traditionally dates to around the middle of the second century (roughly AD 140). The earliest known written form of

---

[1] There exists a curiosity among English Bible translations in that the words Heaven and Hell are not generally capitalized while Paradise, She'ol, and Hádes are fairly consistently capitalized. This could be due to the fact that the latter three are transliterations while the former two are translations. In this work, aside from biblical quotations, these names will be treated as proper nouns when they are used to depict a specific spiritual domain.

the creed appears in a letter that Marcellus of Ancyra wrote to Julius, the bishop of Rome, about AD 341.

To a large degree, the Apostles' Creed echoes the Nicene Creed, which is a longer, more detailed writing that was developed under the auspices of the Roman Emperor Constantine (AD 272-337) at the Council of Nicea in AD 325. The Apostles' Creed, which was devised as a baptismal confession, has undergone some changes since its inception. It originated as what is known as the Old Roman Creed, which read as follows:

> I believe in God the Father almighty;
> and in Christ Jesus His only Son, our Lord,
> Who was born from the Holy Spirit and the Virgin Mary,
> Who under Pontius Pilate was crucified and buried,
> on the third day rose again from the dead,
> ascended into Heaven,
> sits at the right hand of the Father,
> whence he will come to judge the living and the dead;
> and in the Holy Spirit,
> the holy Church,
> the remission of sins,
> the resurrection of the flesh,
> [life everlasting].

The modern-day Apostles' Creed is a slightly expanded version of the Old Roman Creed. That portion of the creed that depicts Jesus descending into Hell was not included in the original text. The words "He descended into Hell" were inserted just after the line concerning Pontius Pilate. How/why did this change occur?

The first known discussion of this addition dates to the late fourth century, at which time a Roman priest by the name of Tyrannius Rufinus of Aquileia (AD 344/345-411) produced a Latin version of the creed known as The Apostles' Creed of Aquileia in AD 390. In that version, he replaced the words "and buried" with the expression *descendit ad inferna* (He descended to Hell). Some modern scholars have suggested that with these words, Rufinus was pointing strictly to Jesus' burial. Yet, he seems to have given mixed messages in his commentary on the creed, offering separately the following two observations:

> 18. They who have handed down the Creed to us have with much forethought specified the time when these things were done — under Pontius Pilate,— lest in any respect the tradition should falter, as though vague and uncertain.

But it should be known that the clause, He descended into Hell, is not added in the Creed of the Roman Church, neither is it in that of the Oriental Churches. It seems to be implied, however, when it is said that He was buried. But in the love and zeal for the Divine Scriptures which possess you, you say to me, I doubt not, These things ought to be proved by more evident testimonies from the Divine Scriptures. For the more important the things are which are to be believed, so much the more do they need apt and undoubted witness.[2]

28. That He descended into Hell is also evidently foretold in the Psalms, where it is said, You have brought Me also into the dust of the death. And again, What profit is there in my blood, when I shall have descended into corruption? And again, I descended into the deep mire, where there is no bottom. Moreover, John says, Are You He that shall come (into Hell, without doubt), or do we look for another? Whence also Peter says that Christ being put to death in the flesh, but quickened in the Spirit which dwells in Him, descended to the spirits who were shut up in prison, who in the days of Noah believed not, to preach unto them; where also what He did in Hell is declared. Moreover, the Lord says by the Prophet, as though speaking of the future, You will not leave my soul in Hell, neither will You suffer Your Holy One to see corruption. Which again, in prophetic language he speaks of as actually fulfilled, O Lord, You have brought my soul out of Hell: You have saved me from them that go down into the pit.[3]

Church leaders continued the conversation concerning *The Descensus* over the next couple of centuries and the terminology was officially inserted into the Apostles' Creed around AD 650. As written in the Greek, the addition read *katelthonta eis ta katôtata* meaning *descended to lower ones*, which could also be translated *descended to those below*. No comparable statement was introduced into the Nicene Creed.

In the early eighth century, a monk by the name of Priminius (approx. AD 670-753) also translated the creed into Latin. Unlike Rufinus and his use of the term *inferna*, Priminius followed the Greek rendering, using the phrase *descendit ad inferos*, which means *descended to the underworld*. It could similarly be translated *descended to those below* (inferior ones). According to Dr. Taylor Marshall:

To be grammatically accurate, the Apostles' Creed is stating that Christ is descending to persons "inferos" and not to a place "infernum," though

---

[2] Rufinus, Tyrannius, Commentary on the Apostles' Creed, *CHURCH FATHERS: Commentary on the Apostles' Creed (Rufinus) (newadvent.org)*, accessed February 14, 2021.
[3] Ibid.

Scripture and Tradition identify the Old Testament righteous souls as waiting in Limbo or "Abraham's Bosom."[4]

So far as is known, the creed was translated into English in the mid-seventeenth century, not long after the introduction of the King James Version of Scripture, and the phrase was translated "He descended into Hell." A convincing argument can be made that, in the KJV, quite often the term for the *realm of the dead* (Heb. *She'ol*, Gr. *Hádes*) was misguidedly translated as *Hell*, and the English translators of the Apostles' Creed seem to have taken their cue from that version of Scripture. In 1988, an ecumenical version was written that was intended to serve as an acceptable translation for all English-speaking churches. In that version, the phrase was changed to "he descended to the dead."

It is fascinating that the doctrine of Jesus descending into Hell has persisted over the past two millennia despite a lack of biblical affirmation. The doctrine leans heavily on inference, extra-biblical sources, and what many see as strained analysis of assorted Bible passages. The perseverance of this doctrine over the centuries can be partly attributed to the fact that the words *He descended into Hell* hold different meanings for different people. Some continue to teach that Jesus descended to Hell while others insist that the phrase is simply a reference to Jesus' descent to either the grave (his burial) or the realm of the dead (Hádes).

What is known about the time Jesus spent in the spiritual world in the days between his death and resurrection? The information is sketchy at best. Still, some information is available from Scripture. The goal here is to use evenhanded reasoning, applying hermeneutic principles as honestly as possible, to draw sound doctrinal views from those Bible passages that offer insight into that spiritual world.

To fully address the topic at hand, it is important to have a reasonable understanding of human death and the spiritual world that lies beyond. Therefore, this discussion begins with an in-depth look into what the Bible has to say about the transition from life to death and how those teachings apply in the case of Jesus' death. This is followed by a methodical review of those passages that ostensibly speak to the notion that Jesus did, indeed, descend into Hell.

---

[4] Marshall, Taylor, *Descended into Hell - Latin and Greek versions of Apostles Creed - Taylor Marshall*, accessed March 6, 2021.

Section 1

Life, Death, And God's Word

Chapter 1
What Scripture Reveals About Death

Introduction of Death

Human death is, by its very nature, foreboding, which is why people generally avoid conversations on this topic. Serious discussions about death generally arise only when necessary (facing terminal illness, etc.). Nevertheless, it is a basic matter where life is concerned, no matter how disconcerting the subject may be.

It is not uncommon for writers to employ the idea of death figuratively, and this is equally true in God's Word. For instance, Paul explained to his readers that as faithful believers, they should consider themselves dead to their previous life of sin (Romans 6: 2, 11; Colossians 2: 20). In similar fashion, Jesus told his followers that anyone who wishes to be his disciple must lose his life (Matthew 16: 24-25). Figurative language can provide a compelling pictorial that touches the mind. However, in this chapter, the focus on death will be more literal.

According to Scripture, men are subject to two kinds of death: physical death and spiritual death. The Bible intimates that death, whether physical or spiritual, involves the separation of two things. Physical death involves separation of one's physical body from his or her spirit (Ecclesiastes 12: 7; James 2: 26). In the case of spiritual death, because of sin, a person is separated (relationally/spiritually) from God (Isaiah 59: 2).

When God created Adam and Eve, he warned them concerning the tree of knowledge of good and evil that he had planted in the Garden of Eden. He told them, "…on the day that you eat from it you will certainly die" (Genesis 2: 17). It is natural for men to presume that God's warning to the couple meant physical death and that it would be instantaneous. Yet, physical death for Adam and Eve did not come immediately.

Since they did not die physically on that day (they had children afterward and Adam lived 930 years), it stands to reason that *instant* physical death was not what God had in mind, although the promise of physical death was certainly couched within his words. Instead, Adam and Eve died spiritually on that day. Their sin separated them from God. They would no longer enjoy an undefiled relationship with him. The lesson that the sinner abides in a state of spiritual death permeates the pages of the New Testament (cf. Colossians 2: 13; Ephesians 2: 1-2). Adam and Eve would eventually experience physical death in keeping with God's warning, but not on the day they sinned.

It can be reasonably inferred from Scripture that physical death is a natural matter where mankind is concerned. The human body, as created, was not designed to live forever without special provision and this principle seems to have applied equally to Adam and Eve prior to their disobedience. Before sin entered the picture, Adam and Eve consumed physical food to sustain life. That is how the human body was fashioned. In fact, food consumption was a key topic in the first recorded conversation between God and Adam (Genesis 1: 29), presumably because of its critical nature, suggesting that it was of utmost importance even in a sinless world.

> **It can be reasonably inferred from Scripture that physical death is a natural matter where mankind is concerned.**

Prior to the fall, Adam and Eve were instructed to eat of any tree in the Garden of Eden except for the tree of knowledge of good and evil, but it was specifically the tree of life that sustained them and prevented death. Had they continued to eat from this tree even after they sinned, they would have continued to live in their physical state forever (Genesis 3: 22). It appears this was a special provision from God aimed at overcoming their limited physical nature. After the fall, God prohibited them from eating of the tree of life (Genesis 3: 24) and their bodies eventually succumbed. This was evidently God's way of fulfilling his promise of death (cf. Romans 5: 12; 6: 23). It seems that, while Adam and Eve did not die physically on the day they sinned, their sin set them on the path to physical death on that day.

Death in the Old Testament

Some have noticed a distinction between the emphases of the Old Testament and New Testament. The focus in the Old Testament seems to be on mankind's physical nature, beginning with God's creation of a physical world. This is evidenced by the fact that God required individual physical animal sacrifices to cover sins and God's chosen people (the Jews) were identified by a physical seed.

When Adam and Eve sinned against God, mankind's relationship with God was altered dramatically, both physically and spiritually. The physical change was realized by the fact that men no longer had the opportunity to live permanently in a physical state. This truth is reflected in the following verses from the book of Ecclesiastes.

> [1]There is an appointed time for everything. And there is a time for every matter under heaven—[2] A time to give birth and a time to die... (Ecclesiastes 3: 1-2)

In the NASV, the word *death* appears roughly 300 times in the Old Testament. Similarly, the words *dead* and *die/died* are used hundreds of times. With very few exceptions, these terms speak to the topic of physical death. The term *grave* is found several dozen times, generally identifying physical graves for those who have died.

The Old Testament emphasis on human physicality can be attributed to the fact that the purpose of the Old Testament is to provide a foundation for the New Testament focus of spiritual life and death. Still, life and death in the context of spirituality is not completely absent from the Old Testament. Consider these allusions to spiritual death from Proverbs.

> In the way of righteousness there is life,
> And in *its* pathway there is no death. (Proverbs 12: 28)

> The fear of the LORD is a fountain of life,
> *By which* one may avoid the snares of death. (Proverbs 14: 27)

Death in the New Testament

In the New Testament, while the term *death* most often points to physical death in the gospels and the book of Acts, there is a distinct shift in the epistles. Beginning with Paul's epistle to the Romans, this word still refers to physical death on several occasions, but there seems to be a much greater emphasis on spiritual life and death or spiritual resurrection. Notice, in the following verses, that death is not weighed against physical life. Rather, death is contrasted with spiritual/eternal life.

> For if by the offense of the one, death reigned through the one, much more will those who receive the abundance of grace and of the gift of righteousness reign in life through the One, Jesus Christ. (Romans 5: 17)

> For the wages of sin is death, but the gracious gift of God is eternal life in Christ Jesus our Lord. (Romans 6: 23)

> We know that we have passed out of death into life, because we love the brothers *and sisters*. The one who does not love remains in death. (1 John 3: 14)

The reason for the shift in emphasis in the New Testament is that the impact of death was diminished dramatically with Jesus' resurrection and the introduction of the gospel message. Through his resurrection, Jesus conquered the consequence of death (both physical and spiritual) as punishment for sin. While people continue to experience physical death, for the believer its effect is ebbed by God's promise of spiritual life beyond the grave.

> But when this perishable puts on the imperishable, and this mortal puts on immortality, then will come about the saying that is written: "DEATH HAS BEEN SWALLOWED UP in victory. (1 Corinthians 15: 54)

> ...but now has been revealed by the appearing of our Savior Christ Jesus, who abolished death and brought life and immortality to light through the gospel (2 Timothy 1: 10)

The Unseen World

Christians see physical death as the separation of an individual's spirit from his/her physical body (cf. John 19: 30). Unbelievers view death as finality – the end of one's existence. If unbelievers are correct, there is nothing more to understand on this topic. The person who has died simply ceases to exist. There are no spiritual consequences. On the other hand, if believers are correct in that, in death, one's spirit is separated from his or her body, it naturally begs the question: *What happens to a person's spirit beyond physical death?*

This work is written based on the premise that the Bible is true, and that the spiritual world described in Scripture does exist; although views differ, even among Christians, when it comes to discerning exactly what happens when one's physical life ends. It is unwise to get too caught up in specific terminology when it comes to the Bible's depiction of death and/or the grave. Not only are different kinds of death in view in God's Word, but the wording is often a mixture of figurative, poetic, prophetic, or apocalyptic language. Consequently, where death is concerned, the phraseology found in a passage of Scripture might not be as significant as some believe. It is better to consider the whole of biblical teaching on the subject than to establish doctrine based on a few select verses.

The voluminous use of the word *spirit* (nearly 400 instances) in the New Testament in its various forms (spirit, spirits, spiritual, Holy Spirit, etc.) offers a powerful statement concerning existence of this spiritual world. However, knowing that a spiritual world exists does not explain the nature of that world. Still, God's Word provides limited insight into the unseen.

The spiritual world is, according to Scripture, a place of rewards and punishments. When a person dies physically, his or her spirit enters this spiritual sphere. Where an individual ultimately lands in that world is dependent upon God's judgment of the life they have lived – whether that person sought to honor God while on earth in a physical state. There are ultimately two final destinations in that world – Heaven and Hell. Yet, these are not the only spiritual domains mentioned in Scripture. Following is a brief examination of the assorted spiritual realms that are revealed in God's Word.

Chapter 2
What Scripture Reveals About Spiritual Domains

Heaven

Heaven is the most notable domain in the unseen world. The Hebrew word *e·shmim* is translated into English as *heaven*, or *the heavens* – a term that appears more than 600 times in the Old Testament. In many of those cases, it is the atmosphere above the earth that is in view with its clouds and rain and sunshine. For instance, the very first verse of Genesis reads, "In the beginning God created the heavens and the earth" (Genesis 1: 1). This is likely a reference not only to the firmament directly above the earth, but to the vastness of space that would hold the planets, the sun, the moon, the stars, and universes that are beyond human capacity to imagine (cf. Isaiah 13: 10).

While the Hebrew *e·shmim* (Gr., *ouranos*) generally points to the physical atmosphere and beyond, other times it serves as a direct reference to God's dwelling place in the spiritual world. That is what is in view in the following passages. It is called "His holy dwelling place…" (2 Chronicles 30: 27) and Jesus told the disciples they should pray, "Our Father, who is in heaven…" (Matthew 6: 9).

It is the Heaven where God dwells with other created spiritual beings (cf. Matthew 18: 10) that is spiritually significant where mankind is concerned. In the New Testament, God has explained that Heaven is a place of spiritual reward for those individuals who are faithful to him – having lived lives that honor him (cf. Matthew 5: 12; Ephesians 1: 3; Colossians 1: 5; 1 Peter 1: 4).

Paradise

A word that is biblically associated with Heaven is *Paradise* (Gr. *paradiesō*). This word appears three times in the New Testament and, in certain contexts, seems to refer to the dwelling place of God that is also called Heaven. Among men, there are assorted views about Paradise and its place in the spiritual realm.

As Jesus hung on the cross, certain convicted criminals shared his fate, hanging on crosses with him at Golgotha. There may have been more than two criminals on crosses that day (cf. Mark 15: 32), but Scripture speaks specifically of two thieves with whom Jesus had at least a small measure of interaction. The detailed story of these thieves is found only in Luke's gospel (Luke 23: 39-43).

While one thief mocked Jesus, the other was humbled, recognizing his own guilt and just punishment while acknowledging Jesus' innocence and the fact that he deserved better than to die on a cross among thieves. These thieves both evidently knew who Jesus was and his claim to be the Messiah, but they had diametrically opposite responses. One of the thieves hurled insults at Jesus while the other simply asked to be remembered when Jesus came into his kingdom.

There is no record of Jesus responding to the man who ridiculed him; although he did answer the thief who had addressed him with all humility, telling the man, "Truly I say to you, today you shall be with Me in Paradise" (Luke 23: 43). The statement reflects Jesus' acknowledgment of the man's honest humility accompanied by a promise that the man would join him in Paradise as they both passed from this earthly life.

Later, evidently writing about his own personal experience/vision, Paul told the Corinthians that "…a man was caught up to the third heaven…caught up into Paradise" (2 Corinthians 12: 2, 4). Also, the Apostle John wrote that the tree of life resides "…in the Paradise of God" (Revelation 2: 7). These two verses indicate that Paradise and Heaven are one or that Paradise is at least a part of Heaven (Paul appears to equate Paradise with "the third heaven").

She'ol/Hádes

She'ol is the Hebrew word that is often used in the Old Testament to depict the idea of death, or the grave. This same idea is expressed in the Greek with the word Hádes. Arguably, the best way to envision She'ol, or Hádes, as discussed in the pages of Scripture, is to define it as the realm of the dead. Information about Hádes is limited, but God's Word does offer some insights. At times, writers use the term narrowly in referring to physical death. Still other times it is used to speak of the unseen world. This is similar to the dual use of *e·shmim* to represent either the physical sky above the earth or God's spiritual home.

There are instances in Scripture when She'ol/Hádes is specifically portrayed as a waiting place for the spirits of the unsaved who have died. This idea is derived from assorted biblical passages like John's words from Revelation concerning the coming judgment, declaring that "…Death and Hádes gave up the dead who were in them; and they were judged" (Revelation 20: 13).

Jesus shared with his disciples a story that lends itself to this view (Luke 16: 19-31). He told them of a rich man and a beggar named Lazarus whom the rich man evidently treated with disdain. When these two men died, Lazarus went to rest in what Jesus identifies as *Abraham's arms* while the rich man found himself in torment in Hádes, at which time there was a conversation between the rich man and Abraham.

Elements of the story have led to a certain amount of speculation. For various reasons, some believe it to be a recounting of a true event while others consider it purely parabolic in character. Some who describe the story of the rich man and Lazarus as strictly a parable believe in what is known as *soul sleep*. The idea behind soul sleep is that when one dies, he/she simply sleeps until Jesus' Second Coming. There is no knowledge or awareness by a person's spirit in death – only sleep. Consequently, the story cannot be a true reflection of the spiritual world.

Others see the story as a true event, or at least one that is illustrative of what lies beyond death, for the following reasons. First, they note that no parable in Scripture uses the *names* of individuals while, in this narrative, Lazarus's name is given. Second, parables use earthly experiences to metaphorically represent spiritual truths. That pattern is not followed in this case since the listener/reader is transported to the spiritual world to witness events that take place there.

The best argument is that, on a basic level, the story is reflective of the spiritual world with which Jesus was so familiar. It seems unlikely that he would intentionally mischaracterize that world, deceiving his disciples. Additionally, every parable Jesus shared was realistic. His parables always described a circumstance that was *possible*. Whether the specific individuals named in the story actually existed is impossible to know, but that is of no consequence since, as with all parables, it is an allegorical depiction of biblical truth.

Whether one believes the story to be parabolic or historical or both has no bearing on the primary lesson Jesus hoped to convey, since the design of the spiritual world is not what Jesus sought to communicate to his followers. What Jesus wanted his listeners to draw from the story of the rich man and Lazarus is that decisions about eternity must be made here – in this life. Once a person has died, their eternal fortune is sealed (Luke 16: 26); nor will they be able to reach out to the loved ones they left behind (Luke 16: 27-31). This is the biblical truth that is advanced in the narrative.

While Jesus' words offer an obscure glimpse into the spiritual world, particularly the domain known as She'ol/Hádes, anything revealed about that world in the narrative is incidental to the storyline. The only thing this episode teaches definitively about She'ol/Hádes is that, according to Jesus, it can refer to a spiritual waiting place for the souls of the lost prior to the final judgment.

Tartarus

Some may wonder about the Apostle Peter's brief reference to a place of apparent spiritual punishment in his second epistle. In this case, the context is a discussion of God's ability to rescue the godly from a sinful world. There is a reference to Hell, but it is given specifically in connection with fallen angels.

> …God did not spare angels when they sinned, but cast them into hell and committed them to pits of darkness, held for judgment. (2 Peter 2: 4)

This is one of the few instances where fallen angels are discussed in God's Word. The text states that God did not spare them, "…but cast them into Hell." In this instance, the word translated as Hell is the Greek *Tartarus*. This verse represents the only use of this word in Scripture, but other Greek literature can help determine what it would have meant to Peter's audience. The word seems to have originated within Greek mythology as a place of punishment. It is mentioned in Homer's Iliad (8th century BC). R. H. Strachan (1873-1958) observed the following:

> In Homer, Hades is the place of confinement of dead men, and Tartarus is the name given to a murky abyss beneath Hades, in which the sins of fallen immortals are punished.[5]

The term was used in similar fashion by Hesiod who, it is believed, may have been a young contemporary of Homer. Plato (BC 427-347) also employed the term Tartarus in like manner in a play he wrote (4th century BC). It is curious that Peter seems to have drawn a term from Greek mythology to discuss spiritual punishment in Scripture.

This use of Tartarus should not be considered Peter's endorsement of mythological beings or places. The apostle's primary point in the surrounding text is that God preserves his followers. Within the framework of that lesson, he uses a term with which his audience would have been familiar to depict an apparent truth – that fallen angels are afforded a special place where they await judgment. He evidently employed the word Tartarus to visualize that message for his readers.

Some may be curious about certain rather shadowy terms that appear in the New Testament that seem to portray the idea of a dreaded spiritual domain. The terms are *the abyss* (Gr. *abysson*), and *the pit* (Gr. *seirais*). These are generally seen as pointing to the likes of Tartarus in the New Testament. In the passage cited at the beginning of this segment (2 Peter 2: 4), the expression "pits of darkness" (Gr. *seirais zophou*; lit., *caverns of darkness*) is the very characterization of Tartarus.

The term *the abyss* seems to be used comparably elsewhere in the New Testament. For instance, in a narrative that depicts Jesus preparing to cast out demons from a possessed man, those demons pleaded with Jesus that he would not send them to the abyss (Luke 8: 31). This suggests a sense of trepidation about the abyss even by these unholy spirits.

In the Old Testament, the term *pit*, or *the pit*, appears several times in various English versions where it is translated from assorted Hebrew words. There it quite often refers to a literal hole in the ground

---

[5] Coffman, J. B., citing R. H. Strachan, *James Burton Coffman Commentaries James 1 & 2 Peter, 1, 2 & 3 John, Jude*, A. C. U. Press, Abilene, TX, 1984, p. 298.

(cf. Psalm 7: 15). Although, when used figuratively, it generally serves as a reference to death or the grave (cf. Job 33: 18).

Hell

The very idea of Hell is a bit disconcerting. It is assumed by many that the English word *Hell* is derived from the Saxon word *helan*, which means *to cover* or *to conceal*. Those who believe in the truth of Scripture realize that Hell represents the ultimate fate/punishment for those who have not accepted Jesus as their personal savior. Even unbelievers understand what the word represents. They recognize that, if Hell is real, it is a place to be avoided.

The use of this word in Scripture can be misleading since there are times in English Bible translations where it is incorrectly applied. For instance, in certain English translations, the word Hell does not appear in the Old Testament writings. This is true of the ASV, ESV, HCSB, NASV, NIV, NRSV, RSV, and others. Compare these to other Old Testament English translations such as the KJV, where it appears thirty-one times, the NKJV, where it is used nineteen times, and the 1599 Geneva Bible, where this translation can be found twenty-one times.

It seems odd that this word, which appears thirty-one times in the KJV of the Old Testament, would be absent from a multitude of other translations, but there is a reason for this. The word the King James translators chose to depict as Hell is the Hebrew *She'ol*, which was discussed a bit earlier. Despite the KJV translation, it is important to recognize that She'ol/Hádes is not Hell. Jeremy Myers and Timothy Lewis respectively make the following observations:

> The word *sheol* occurs sixty-six times in the Hebrew Scriptures, and a few of these are occasionally translated as "hell" depending on which Bible translation you are reading. Yet "hell" is not a good translation of any of the occurrences of *sheol* in the Bible. The Hebrew bible never indicates any form of punishment after death, so this translation is inappropriate.[6]
>
> ...the translation of Sheol as "hell" was indeed a result of cultural imposition, a consequence of the seventeenth-century's fascination with hell.[7]

---

[6] Myers, Jeremy, *What is Sheol? What is Hell?* (redeeminggod.com), accessed March 3, 2021.
[7] Lewis, Timothy, *Translating Sheol as "Hell": A Clear Case of Cultural Imposition?* (DOC) Translating Sheol as "Hell": A Clear Case of Cultural Imposition? | Timothy Lewis – Academia.edc, accessed March 3, 2021.

If She'ol does not mean Hell, even though it is a reference to the realm of the dead, then what *is* Hell? The term that is generally translated into English as Hell is the Greek word *Gehenna*. This word, as it appears in the New Testament, was transliterated from the Aramaic form of the Hebrew *ge-hinnom*, "valley of Hinnom." What is the origin of the word? According to Easton's Bible Dictionary:

> **Gehenna** [N] [B] [S]
> (originally Ge bene Hinnom; i.e., "the valley of the sons of Hinnom"), a deep, narrow glen to the south of Jerusalem, where the idolatrous Jews offered their children in sacrifice to Molech (2 Chronicles 28:3; 33:6; Jeremiah 7:31; 19:2-6). This valley afterwards became the common receptacle for all the refuse of the city. Here the dead bodies of animals and of criminals, and all kinds of filth, were cast and consumed by fire kept always burning. It thus in process of time became the image of the place of everlasting destruction. In this sense it is used by our Lord in Matthew 5:22 Matthew 5:29 Matthew 5:30; 10:28; 18:9; Matthew 23:15 Matthew 23:33; Mark 9:43 Mark 9:45 Mark 9:47 ; Luke 12:5. In these passages, and also in James 3:6 , the word is uniformly rendered "hell," the Revised Version placing "Gehenna" in the margin.[8]

The New Testament concept of Hell as a place of eternal spiritual punishment is not specifically discussed in the Old Testament. Nevertheless, the absence of this teaching in the Old Testament should not be seen as an opportunity to discount New Testament instruction. The doctrine of God's wrath toward and inevitable judgment of unfaithful people is clear in both testaments.

The term *Gehenna* is found only a dozen times in the New Testament – mostly in the gospels of Matthew, Mark, and Luke where, each time it appears, the writer is quoting Jesus. The only exception is a verse from the book of James where it is used in conjunction with the evil deeds of the tongue (James 3: 6). Generally, it is depicted as a place of spiritual punishment.

Although the word *Gehenna* does not appear in the book of Revelation, Hell is discussed there. In that work, instead of calling it by its common name, the apostle has depicted it as a "lake of fire" (Revelation 19: 20; 20: 14-15). Yet, there is no mistaking the descriptive term "lake of fire" as anything else. It is an incontrovertible reference to Hell. The description of Hell as *fiery hell* or a *place of fire* is found in a number of New Testament passages (cf. Matthew 5: 22; Mark 9: 43).

---

[8] https://www.biblestudytools.com/dictionary/Gehenna/, accessed July 4, 2019.

Scripture portrays Hell as the place of final judgment/punishment not only for fallen other-worldly beings, such as fallen angels, but for unfaithful human beings – those whose names are "...not found written in the book of life" (Revelation 20: 15) – as well. That having been said, there is no indication in God's Word that anyone has, as of this writing, been cast into Hell. It is not a place to which souls automatically journey upon physical death. Those who will not spend eternity with God are, according to Scripture, "...thrown into the lake of fire" (Revelation 20: 10, 14, 15) following the final day of judgment. These words reflect a deliberate and decisive future act of God rather than an immediate consequence of death.

Jesus alluded to or spoke directly of Hell, depicting it as a place of consuming fire (cf. Matthew 3: 10, 12; 5: 22; 7: 19; 19: 8; Mark 9: 43-49). However, since it exists in the spiritual realm, humankind may not be able to grasp its true nature. Consequently, biblical descriptions of Hell may simply be God's way of explaining the spiritual world in human terms for people who only understand the physical environment that surrounds them. Based on what little information is available from Scripture, it can be concluded that it is a place of post-death spiritual punishment. Since Scripture offers no further details, much of what people claim to know or believe about the nature of Hell is speculative.

The Unknowable

The design of the spiritual world, with assorted domains and spiritual beings, is beyond the comprehension of the human mind. Only bits and pieces are offered in Scripture, such as those occasions when angels have appeared to men. These provide an opaque glimpse into that world, but they are insufficient for people to successfully envision the spiritual domains or the events that occur there. The biblical words used to depict that world (e.g., lake of fire, abyss, etc.) fail to explain anything except that the spiritual world is vastly different from the physical world of humankind.

While the Bible affords mankind limited insight into the unseen world, many questions remain unanswered. This is undoubtedly intentional on God's part since he has declared salvation to be a matter of faith – believing in and relying on that which is not fully known or fully seen. This is the very definition of faith according to Scripture (Hebrews 11: 1).

Men cannot see the wind, but they see evidence of its presence in the movement of the leaves on the trees, and feel it against their skin, etc. Similarly, while people cannot visibly behold the unseen world, God has provided sufficient evidence for them, through faith, to accept its existence. If humankind were given complete information about, or unbridled contact with, that world, the idea of *faith* as a matter of salvation would lose its meaning. Therefore, God has provided enough information for people to have faith without offering so much information that it would be impossible to live by faith.

Chapter 3

What Scripture Reveals About Soul and Spirit

Creation

The story of creation is generally well-known, even among those who profess to believe in the theory of evolution. Most people are familiar with the first few verses of Genesis where the beginning of creation is memorialized. The first day of creation saw God bring into being an initial draft of the earth and the heavens to which he added light and darkness (Genesis 1: 1-5).

Over the next several days following this initial act, God added to his wonder of creation. On the second day, he separated the earth from the sky (Genesis 1: 6-8). The next day he separated the land from the waters. That same day, God brought forth all kinds of vegetation on the face of the earth (Genesis 1: 9-13). On the fourth day, God placed the sun and moon in the sky to give light on earth. Along with these two he added to the expanse of the heavens with more stars and planets (Genesis 1: 14-19). God had already added life to his creation with the introduction of vegetation. However, on the fifth day, he brought forth "...every living creature that moves" (v. 21). This involved the formation of creatures in the water and birds of the air (Genesis 1: 21-23).

While every day of the creation process is significant, these first five days can be regarded as steps that were taken in preparation for the sixth day. With the creation of the earth, vegetation, the sun and moon, sea creatures, and birds of flight, it was time for an extraordinary step. On the sixth day, he brought forth all kinds of animals who would dwell on the land, including "...livestock and crawling things and animals of the earth according to their kind" (v. 24). The words *according to their (or its) kind* is a phrase repeated no less than seven times over the five verses that speak to this phase of creation. The implication from the text is that animals were created male and female with the intent of perpetuating each species.

These things God did, readying for the *crème de la crème* of his masterpiece. His plan was to create a being in his own image. The balance of the first chapter of God's Word tells the story of the creation of humankind. That story is further detailed in the second chapter of Genesis. The climax of the creation process is found in the following verse.

> And the LORD God formed man of the dust of the ground, and breathed into his nostrils the breath of life; and man became a living soul. (Genesis 2: 7, KJV)

One word in this verse deserves additional consideration since it has been the source of much discussion and confusion. It is the Hebrew word *nephesh,* rendered "soul" in the KJV cited here. Many people wonder about the meaning of this word with respect to human life, particularly when it is juxtaposed against the Hebrew word *ruach,* which is generally translated *spirit* in the Old Testament (cf. Numbers 16: 22; 27: 16), often referring to man's spiritual essence. The question often arises: *Do soul and spirit carry the same meaning or is each a distinct matter where a human life is concerned?*

The larger conversation from which this specific question arises involves varying beliefs about the full nature of humankind. There are three main viewpoints on the subject. The first is *monism,* which states that the human life exists only in a single, physical state. Mental and emotional ingredients of life are simply extensions of the physical state that have developed through the evolutionary process in response to surrounding stimuli.

The second view is called *dichotomy* (a.k.a., anthropological dualism) where a human being is understood to exist in both a physical and a spiritual state in tandem, these constituting two metaphysically distinct, yet complementary, states of being. The third and final view is known as *trichotomy*. Those who profess this view insists that a human being is composed of a material presence (physical body), a psychological element (soul), and a spiritual essence (spirit). Some believe one's mentality is centered in the soul while others teach that one's spirit is the ruler of intellect and that persona (individuality and emotional passions) derives from the soul.

Those who accept the Genesis creation account, and the teachings of the Bible, will dismiss *monism* with prejudice.[9] Since Adam's physical body was created from the dust of the ground but did not take on life until he received the breath of life, the monistic position collapses under the weight of the evidence. This, however, does not address questions concerning the immaterial (unseen) human elements of soul and/or spirit. Much of the confusion on this topic derives from various biblical translations that can leave one a bit perplexed. Add to this the fact that, at times, these terms are applied differently in different biblical settings, and puzzlement can be the result.

Soul

The Hebrew term *nephesh*, in its various forms (noun, adjective, singular, plural, etc.), appears more than seven hundred times in the Old Testament. Depending on the specific Bible version, it has been translated into a wide selection of English words. For instance, in the KJV, *nephesh* is often translated as *soul* while, in the NIV, this word is interpreted using more than one hundred different English words depending on the context. The KJV, published in 1611, uses *soul* in the Old Testament more than four hundred times. The NIV, published in the twentieth century, pales in comparison since, in that translation, *soul* appears less than one hundred times in the Old Testament. The NASV, also published in the twentieth century, uses the term *soul* just under two hundred fifty times in the Old Testament.

These differences can easily be attributed to interpretive preference, but it does make it more difficult to nail down the precise meaning of a word that so many see so differently. Nevertheless, there is some commonality in the use of this word, particularly with respect to human

---

[9] In legal terms, a case dismissed *with prejudice* means that the cause of action, or lawsuit, is closed for good.

life. That trend seems to complement the use of *nephesh* in the record of creation.

When God breathed into Adam *the breath of life*, "...man became a living soul" (Genesis 2: 7, KJV). The idea behind these words is easy to follow. The verse states simply that man *took on* life...he became a living *being*. The NASV translates nephesh as *person* while the NIV renders it as *being* in this verse.

Interestingly, there are occasions in the Old Testament where the context of *nephesh* does seem to point to something distinctly spiritual in nature. In these passages, the word appears to point to the spiritual essence of an individual. The first records a woman's death while the second depicts Elijah raising a boy from the dead by asking the Lord to return the boy's *nephesh* to his body. The third specifically distinguishes between soul and body.

> It came about as her soul (nephesh) was departing (for she died), that she named him Ben-oni; but his father called him Benjamin. (Genesis 35: 18)

> [21] Then he stretched himself out over the boy three times, and called to the LORD and said, "LORD, my God, please, let this boy's life (nephesh) return to him." [22] And the LORD listened to the voice of Elijah, and the life (nephesh) of the boy returned to him and he revived. (1 Kings 17: 21-22)

> And He will destroy the glory of his forest and of his fruitful garden, both soul (nephesh) and body, And it will be as when a sick person wastes away. (Isaiah 10: 18)

The word in the New Testament that is commonly translated as *soul* is the Greek word *psuche*. From this word come English words such as *psyche* and *psychology*. This fact might lead one to believe that *psuche* is primarily meant to depict mental awareness, but that is not necessarily the case.

To some degree, *psuche* in the New Testament is used to portray human life, or personage, in much the same way that *nephesh* is used in the Old Testament. This is the case in the following verses where a translation of *people* would render a similar meaning.

> So then, those who had received his word were baptized; and that day there were added about three thousand souls (psuche). (Acts 2: 41)

> [13]...They count it a pleasure to revel in the daytime. They are stains and blemishes, reveling in their deceptions as they feast with you, [14] having eyes

full of adultery that never cease from sin, enticing unstable souls (psuche), having hearts trained in greed, accursed children... (2 Peter 2: 13-14).

While *psuche* does take on this meaning on occasion, there are other times in the New Testament when it is plainly meant to portray the spiritual nature of a human being.

> Do not fear those who kill the body but are unable to kill the soul (psuche); but rather fear Him who is able to destroy both soul (psuche) and body in hell. (Matthew 10: 28)

> Now may the God of peace Himself sanctify you entirely; and may your spirit and soul (psuche) and body be preserved complete, without blame at the coming of our Lord Jesus Christ. (1 Thessalonians 5: 23)

With Scripture as guide, it can be reasonably established that the Greek *psuche* should be considered synonymous with the Hebrew *nephesh*. They are both used in a dual capacity to depict one's personage as a human being and, separately and distinctly, a person's unseen spiritual nature.

It is notable that the Thessalonians passage cited here mentions both *soul* and *spirit*, seemingly distinguishing between them. This verse is one source that has led some to believe in the *trichotomy* view of human life mentioned early in the chapter. Therefore, careful consideration of the Bible's presentation of *spirit* is necessary to clarify the nature of the relationship between the human *soul* and the human *spirit*.

Spirit

The Hebrew word that is most often translated as *spirit* in the Old Testament is *ruach*. It appears hundreds of times in the Old Testament and, like *nephesh*, this word has an assortment of English translations depending on the specific context in which it is used. For instance, much of the time this word is used to identify the spirit of God (cf. Genesis 1: 2; Exodus 31: 3; 35: 31; Numbers 11: 26; 24: 2; Psalm 51: 11; 143: 10). In these settings, *ruach* generally points to the Holy Spirit who is identified biblically as the third member of the Godhead (cf. Matthew 28: 19). Other times it simply describes God's demeanor, as a spiritual being, in his relationship with humankind.

> Then the LORD said, "My Spirit (ruach) will not remain with man forever, because he is also flesh; nevertheless his days shall be 120 years." (Genesis 6: 3)

It might be argued that, on rare occasion, the term is used to identify an *evil* spirit (Judges 9: 23; 1 Samuel 16: 14-23; 18: 10; 19: 9; 2 Chronicles 18: 21-22; Zechariah 13: 2). While the term *evil/unclean spirit* appears in English translations in these passages, a strong argument can be made, based on the original language, that the author may not have had other-worldly beings in view. It could be that these references are not to actual evil spirits, but to a spirit of contention, jealousy, or anger. Consider the following text from Judges.

> Then God sent an evil spirit (ruach) between Abimelech and the leaders of Shechem; and the leaders of Shechem dealt treacherously with Abimelech. (Judges 9: 23)

It is reasonable to believe that, in the original language, this may have been intended as a figurative application of the expression *evil spirit* in this context. Here are the thoughts offered in certain commentaries concerning the evil spirit mentioned in this verse.

> Then God sent an evil spirit between Abimelech and the men of Shechem – i.e., in the course of Providence, jealousy, distrust, secret disaffection, and smothered rebellion appeared among his subjects, disappointed and disgusted with his tyranny; and God permitted those disorders to punish the complicated crimes of the royal fratricide and idolatrous usurper.[10]

> He permitted jealousies to take place which produced factions; and these factions produced insurrections, civil contentions, and slaughter.[11]

These commentaries suggest, and perhaps rightfully so, that the *evil spirit* mentioned here was not a literal evil being from the spirit world, but an attitude (spirit) of jealousy, frustration, and anger. It seems more in line with God's character that he would *allow* animosity to build between the characters rather than actively *insert* an evil spiritual being

---

[10] Jamieson, Robert, Faussett, A. R., Brown, David, *A Commentary on the Old and New Testaments*, Hendrickson Publishers, Inc., Peabody, MA, 2008, p. 98.
[11] Clark, Adam, *Clarke's Commentary Volume II: Joshua-Esther*, Abingdon-Cokesbury Press. New York-Nashville, p 143.

into this setting. The same could be said of other verses in the Old Testament where the term *evil spirit* appears.

Some commentators disagree with this assessment, insisting that the reference is to evil members of the spirit world. If, however, these verses are intended to depict actual evil spirits, that use of *ruach* is extremely scarce in the Old Testament.

Quite often in the Old Testament, *ruach* is specifically used to convey the idea of attitude or character. Phrases like "spirit of jealousy" (Numbers 5: 14, NASV 1995 Edition), "spirit of wisdom" (Deuteronomy 34: 9), "they were in high spirits" (Judges 16: 25), or "despairing in spirit" (1 Samuel 1: 15), are not uncommon. In the Psalms and Proverbs are found phrases like "steadfast spirit" (Psalm 51: 10), "willing spirit" (Psalm 51: 12), "broken spirit" (Psalm 51: 17), "haughty spirit" (Proverbs 16: 18) and "humble spirit" (Proverbs 29: 23). This use of *ruach* appears regularly in Old Testament writings.

There are other semi-common uses of *ruach*. For instance, in certain settings it is rendered *wind* in English translations (cf. Genesis 8: 1; Exodus 10: 13; Psalm 1: 4). Other times it is translated into English as *breath* in relation to the breath men breathe, sometimes with a hint of spiritual essence present in the text.

> Remember that my life is a *mere* breath (ruach). (Job 7: 7)

> [3] For as long as life is in me,
> And the breath (ruach) of God is in my nostrils,
> [4] My lips certainly will not speak unjustly,
> Nor will my tongue mutter deceit. (Job 27: 3-4)

Although it occurs less often, there are instances in the Old Testament when *ruach* addresses the unseen spiritual essence of humanity, much like *nephesh* (translated as soul), which was discussed earlier. The following verses demonstrate this use of *ruach*.

> Will You perform wonders for the dead? Or will the departed spirits (ruach) rise *and* praise You? *Selah* (Psalms 88: 10)

> ...then the dust will return to the earth as it was, and the spirit (ruach) will return to God who gave it. (Ecclesiastes 12: 7)

> The dead will not live, the departed spirits (ruach) will not rise. (Isaiah 26: 14)

There is a noticeable commonality present in these uses of *ruach*. It generally represents that which is unseen. Sometimes it is a reference to the spiritual world, to which human access is quite limited. Other times it represents those things in the physical world (breath, wind, etc.) that are simply invisible to the human eye.

Because the Old Testament focuses primarily on the physical world, the Hebrew words *nephesh* and *ruach* are seldom used to specifically identify mankind's spiritual essence. Most often *nephesh* is used to portray life in general rather than the strictly spiritual essence of human life, and *ruach* is largely used to identify either the Holy Spirit (cf. Genesis 1: 2; Isaiah 63: 10), or the character and/or demeanor of mankind as noted in this chapter.

The word that is generally translated into English as *spirit* in the New Testament is the Greek word *pneuma*. As with *ruach* in the Old Testament, *pneuma* is translated into English using various terms such as *breath*, *wind*, etc. Of nearly four hundred appearances in the New Testament, on well over three hundred of those occasions, *pneuma* is translated as *spirit* in most English translations.

In the gospels (Matthew, Mark, Luke, and John), there are many references to the Holy Spirit. This term is also used, often by Jesus, to represent human character. In the Sermon on the Mount, he spoke of "…the poor in spirit" (meek) who would inherit the Kingdom of Heaven (Matthew 5: 3). On a separate occasion, Jesus noted the willingness of one's spirit to do God's will, but the weakness of the flesh to overcome temptation (Matthew 26: 41). Similarly, John recounts that Jesus was "…moved in spirit" (John 11: 33) and "…troubled in spirit" (John 13: 21).

Matthew and John each note that, when Jesus died, his spirit left his body (Matthew 27: 50; John 19: 30), and Luke quotes Jesus as he spoke from the cross, "Father, INTO YOUR HANDS I ENTRUST MY SPIRIT." (Luke 23: 46). These verses from Matthew, Luke, and John distinguish between Jesus' physical and spiritual states as his spirit left his body at the time of death. There are also, in the gospels, several references to evil/unclean spirits who possessed human beings. On occasion, Jesus cast out demons from those who were possessed (cf. Matthew 8: 16; Mark 1: 23-26; 5: 2-13; Luke 7: 21; 9: 37-43).

It is in the book of Acts where Scripture slowly begins to shift focus toward things spiritual. That is because this work follows the transition from the Abrahamic covenant of the Old Testament to the fulfillment of the promises of that covenant in the establishment of the church. Consequently, Acts follows very closely the work of the Holy Spirit, particularly in conjunction with the lives of the apostles, as the church was founded. For instance, spiritual gifts were introduced originally to the apostles (Acts 2: 1-4), the indwelling presence of the Holy Spirit was made available to believers (Acts 2: 38), and the apostles, through the laying on of hands, distributed the power of the Holy Spirit to other believers, resulting in spiritual gifts (Acts 8: 17).

The term *pneuma* appears many times in Acts, most often identifying the Holy Spirit. It also occasionally identifies evil spirits (cf. Acts 5: 16; 8: 7; 16: 8; 19: 12-16). On at least one occasion, *pneuma* speaks to the dual physical and spiritual state of a man. As he was being stoned to death, Stephen "…called on *the Lord* and said, 'Lord Jesus, receive my spirit!'" (Acts 7: 59). This is reminiscent of the words Jesus spoke from the cross as recorded by Luke.

It is in the epistles where teaching about the spiritual essence of humankind, as well as insight into the spiritual world, comes into greater focus. For example, *pneuma* is specifically recognized as that part of man the connects with the Holy Spirit (Romans 8: 16). Also, *pneuma* is identified as the part of human nature that transcends the physical state (1 Corinthians 5: 5; 7: 34). In his letter, James even distinguishes between the human spirit and the human body (James 2: 26).

Paul introduced the idea of eternal life to the believers in Rome (Romans 6: 23). Quite often, in the epistles, Paul's emphasis is on living spiritually, understanding that believers no longer belong to this physical world. That is because the Holy Spirit lives within the believer on a spiritual plane (cf. Romans 5: 5; 1 Corinthians 6: 19; 2 Timothy 1: 14).

Paul's letters contain extensive teaching about the spiritual world to which believers will transition beyond this earthly dwelling. For instance, his first epistle to the Corinthians offers instruction concerning the mystery of resurrection and insight into the imperishable bodies of the resurrected in the spiritual world contrasted against the perishable bodies of this world (1 Corinthians 15: 42-54). Similarly, Peter briefly addresses the nature of the imperishable life that is reserved in Heaven for the faithful (1 Peter 1: 4, 23).

From the Apostle Paul, the Thessalonians learned the facts about resurrection from the dead to a spiritual life and the truth that believers will go to live with Christ forever when they pass from this physical life

(1 Thessalonians 4: 13-17). Jesus will return to claim his own on what Paul terms "...the day of the Lord" (1 Thessalonians 5: 2).

His letter to the Philippians finds Paul looking forward to a time when he would leave this earthly veil and go to be with Christ (Philippians 1: 21-23). A similar message concerning the eternal spiritual life that awaits is found in letters to some of his closest disciples (1 Timothy 4: 8; Titus 1: 2).

Eternal spiritual life that awaits the faithful is thematic not only in John's gospel letter, but in his first epistle. The expression *eternal life* appears six times in five chapters in the epistle of 1 John. In fact, this phrase appears more than forty times in the New Testament. Since it has been established unequivocally that eternal life is granted to mankind's spiritual being, it can be said that the distinct spiritual state of mankind is well established in the New Testament.

Dichotomy vs Trichotomy

The primary question remains concerning soul and spirit. Of the views mentioned early in the chapter – dichotomy or trichotomy – which one is supported by Scripture? Are soul and spirit distinct unseen states of being, or are they one? The best answer is that God's Word presents mankind as dualistic in nature (dichotomy). A human being consists of a physical essence and a spiritual essence. The fact that *nephesh* and *psuche* are at times used to identify life as a whole or are seemingly distinguishable from one's spirit can be confusing, but context is the key to understanding these instances. An explanation of the following texts should help.

> Now may the God of peace Himself sanctify you entirely; and may your spirit and soul and body be preserved complete, without blame at the coming of our Lord Jesus Christ. (1 Thessalonians 5: 23)

> [12] For the word of God is living and active, and sharper than any two-edged sword, even penetrating as far as the division of soul and spirit, of both joints and marrow, and able to judge the thoughts and intentions of the heart. (Hebrews 4: 12)

Some teach that Paul's use of "spirit and soul and body" in his letter to the Thessalonians provides an undeniable biblical portrait of trichotomy. The verse, it is said, clearly identifies three individual members that, together, comprise a human life. Although this approach to the text is understandable, it is probably not the best explanation for Paul's statement when weighed against the balance of God's Word.

In both the Old and New Testaments, *soul* is often presented as synonymous with *spirit* when it comes to the nature of mankind. For instance, in Genesis, a woman died when her soul departed (Genesis 35: 18). Yet, several Old Testament passages identify the spiritual essence of the dead as *departed spirits* (cf. Job 26: 5; Psalm 88: 10; Isaiah 26: 14, 19). Similarly, in the New Testament, when Jesus spoke of the human soul, he clearly had a person's spiritual essence – that which survives physical death – in view (cf. Matthew 10: 28; 16: 26). In like manner, just as Peter wrote of the purification of the soul (1 Peter 1: 22), Paul wrote of the cleansing of body and spirit (2 Corinthians 7: 1).

The equal treatment of soul and spirit throughout Scripture when portraying the nature of mankind cannot be ignored. Paul simply waxes poetic in the Thessalonians text (above). His point is not to differentiate between spirit, soul, and body, but to emphasize the entire person. Jesus similarly stated, "YOU SHALL LOVE THE LORD YOUR GOD WITH ALL YOUR HEART, AND WITH ALL YOUR SOUL, AND WITH ALL YOUR MIND" (MATTHEW 22: 37). The terms *heart*, *soul*, and *mind* are not given to distinguish between them, but to accentuate the complete man. The same is true in the Thessalonians text.

> **The equal treatment of soul and spirit throughout Scripture when portraying the nature of mankind cannot be ignored.**

Where the text from Hebrews is concerned, the verse not only fails to distinguish between soul and spirit, but it goes far to confirm oneness where these terms are concerned. The word translated "penetrating" (Gr. *diiknoumenos*) means *to pierce*. This is not a portrayal of God's Word *separating* two objects but *splitting* one object (soul/spirit). That is the very idea behind this word. A sword that slides between two objects has pierced nothing but the air.

Consider, for a moment, the comment concerning "joints and marrow." If the idea is to separate two items, the verse might read *bones and marrow*. A joint consists of bones, marrow, and cartilage. The marrow is as much a part of the joint as the bones and cartilage. If the marrow is removed, it is no longer the joint God created since only bones and cartilage remain.

Also consider the expression "the thoughts and intentions of the heart." This phrase helps demonstrate the thought process behind these remarks. Just as the power of God's Word can divide soul and spirit, which are one, or joints and marrow, which are one, so he can judge thoughts and intentions, which are indivisible from a human perspective. The author's intent is not to distinguish between soul and spirit, but to picture for his audience the penetrating power of the word of God.

Chapter 4
What Scripture Reveals About Resurrection

Perishable vs Imperishable

Scripture distinguishes between a resurrected *imperishable* spiritual body and a *perishable* physical body. The difference is illustrated in the Apostle Paul's remarks contrasting Jesus' resurrected state and Adam's created state (1 Corinthians 15: 42-45). The natural (physical) life is described as preceding spiritual (eternal) life, a distinction characterized as "…those who are earthy and…those who are heavenly" (1 Corinthians 15: 48). In the transition from the natural to the spiritual "…this perishable must put on the imperishable, and this mortal *must* put on immortality" (1 Corinthians 15: 53).

Nothing in Paul's words suggests that a change took place with respect to mankind's physical nature once sin entered the world. Rather, the narrative indicates that perishable physicality was an innate characteristic of humanity. With the introduction of sin, human access to the tree of life was removed. Without the tree of life, absent godly intercession, physical death for mankind became inevitable.

Resurrection from the dead is discussed at length in God's Word. Even prior to his death, this was a serious topic of discussion as Jesus predicted his own resurrection to his disciples (cf. Matthew 20: 17-19). Also, Jesus raised Jairus's daughter from the dead (Luke 8: 40-56) as well as his close friend Lazarus (John 11: 1-44). Later, when Jesus died on the cross, Scripture reveals that a host of saints were raised again to life (Matthew 27: 52-53).

Some are bewildered by the teaching that saints were raised when Jesus died on the cross, insisting that, while Scripture indicates that their graves may have been opened when Jesus died, the people must not have woken from death until after Jesus' resurrection. They insist that this must be the case since God's Word identifies Jesus as "...the first fruits of those who are asleep" (1 Corinthians 15: 20). This statement, it is said, means that Jesus was the first to be raised in an imperishable body. However, the fact that Jesus was the first to be raised in an *imperishable* state should not be confused with the idea that he was the first human being to be raised from the dead.

Types of Resurrection

In the Old Testament, God's Word recounts the resurrection of certain individuals. These include the son of the Zeraphath woman (1 Kings 17: 17-22), the son of a Shunammite woman (2 Kings 4: 32-35), and a man whose body touched Elisha's bones (2 Kings 13: 20-21). Beyond those already discussed, the New Testament mentions a few others who were raised from the dead including the son of a widow of Nain (Luke 7: 11-15), Dorcas of Joppa (Acts 9: 36-41), and Eutychus, the young man who fell from the window while Paul was speaking (Acts 20: 9-10).

Of interest is the fact that only Eutychus and Dorcas were raised from the dead after Jesus' resurrection. What, then, did Paul mean when describing Jesus as "...the first fruits of those who are asleep" (1 Corinthians 15: 20)? The answer to this question lies in the fact that different *types* of resurrections are depicted in the Bible. Specifically, Scripture identifies two types of resurrection from human death.

There is every reason to believe that those who were raised from the dead in the Old Testament continued to live in their resurrected bodies just as Jesus did, but only for a time. Their human bodies eventually failed, and they were once again given over to physical death. The same can be said of those who, in the New Testament, rose from the dead. Jesus, it seems, is the exception to this rule, and it is this distinction to which Paul was pointing when he wrote of Jesus' resurrected body.

> [14] For if we believe that Jesus died and rose *from the dead*, so also God will bring with Him those who have fallen asleep through Jesus. [15] For we say this to you by the word of the Lord, that we who are alive and remain until the coming of the Lord, will not precede those who have fallen asleep. [16] For the Lord Himself will descend from heaven with a shout, with the voice of *the* archangel and with the trumpet of God, and the dead in Christ will rise first. [17] Then we who are alive, who remain, will be caught up together with them in the clouds to meet the Lord in the air, and so we will always be with the Lord. (1 Thessalonians 4: 14-17)

When Jesus returns to claim his own, he "…will bring with Him those who have fallen asleep through Jesus" (v. 14). In other words, those faithful who died prior to Christ's return will return *with* him. This truth, coupled with Paul's claim that, were he to die, he would be with Christ (Philippians 1: 21-24), indicates that those who have died in Christ have gone to be with him. However, the Thessalonians text also states that Jesus will return "…with a shout, with the voice of *the* archangel and with the trumpet of God, and the dead in Christ will rise first" (v. 16). If the dead in Christ are raised at the time of Jesus' coming, how can this be reconciled with Paul's claim that, upon death, he would be with Christ (Philippians 1: 21-24)?

The human body in its earthly state is not designed to enter the spiritual world. Paul explained this to the Corinthians and Philippians as he expounded on the believer's eventual transformation from a natural physical state to a glorified spiritual state that was exemplified in Christ's resurrection.

> [50] Now I say this, brothers *and sisters*, that flesh and blood cannot inherit the kingdom of God; nor does the perishable inherit the imperishable. [51] Behold, I am telling you a mystery; we will not all sleep, but we will all be changed, [52] in a moment, in the twinkling of an eye, at the last trumpet; for the trumpet will sound, and the dead will be raised imperishable, and we will be changed. [53] For this perishable must put on the imperishable, and this mortal *must* put on immortality. (1 Corinthians 15: 50-53)

> [20] For our citizenship is in heaven, from which we also eagerly wait for a Savior, the Lord Jesus Christ; [21] who will transform the body of our lowly condition into conformity with His glorious body, by the exertion of the power that He has even to subject all things to Himself. (Philippians 3: 20-21)

When Jesus rose from the grave, he rose in a body unlike the bodies of others who were raised from the dead. Eutychus, Dorcas, and others were raised in *perishable* bodies like unto the created body of Adam. Their resurrected bodies were still subject to illness and death. Comparatively, Jesus was raised in an *imperishable* spiritual body suited for Heaven. He still had the scars of the nails in his hands (John 20: 27), but his body was changed from a natural state to a resurrected spiritual state. This explains why he was able to ascend to Heaven a few weeks after his resurrection (Acts 1: 9). McGarvey and Pendleton have explained this bodily distinction with the following words.

> Man in his fleshly nature has no place in heaven, for corruption is antagonistic to incorruption, as light is to darkness. It is essential, therefore, that man must put off the corruption of Adam and the natural body of Adam, and assume the incorruptible, spiritual body of Christ before he can enter his celestial inheritance.[12]

Much has been said about Jesus' resurrected state and some have insisted that he arose in the *exact* same physical state in which he died. After all, he seems to have denied being only a spirit and he claimed to have flesh and bone (Luke 24: 39). When he was offered food, he took it and ate (Luke 24: 41-42). He even offered Thomas the opportunity to reach out and touch the scars in his hands (John 20: 27). These words from the gospels must be weighed against Paul's words to the Corinthians and Philippians where he differentiates between Christ's natural and resurrected body.

Jesus physically rose from the grave and lived in his resurrected body. Scripture is clear on that fact. However, the Bible also calls it a *glorified* state (cf. John 7: 39). His resurrected body was suited for entrance into the spiritual domain of Heaven (cf. Acts 1: 9), which is not true of a natural human body. Paul refers to this kind of transformation as a mystery (1 Corinthians 15: 51). Matt Slick and John Piper each seem to have captured the essence of this mystery.

> Jesus rose from the dead in the very same physical body in which He died. This resurrected, physical body was a glorified, spiritual body. The spiritual body is not merely "spirit." The spiritual body is the resurrected, glorified, physical body.[13]

---

[12] McGarvey, J. W. and Pendleton, Philip Y., *A Commentary on Thessalonians, Corinthians, Galatians, and Romans*, Gospel Light Publishing, Delight, AR, p. 158.
[13] Slick, Matt, *Jesus' Resurrection was Physical*, Christian Apologetics and Research Ministry, https://carm.org/jesus-resurrection-was-physical, accessed May 23, 2020.

The body will be raised from the dead, and the bodily resurrection of Jesus in a form that could be recognized and that could be touched and that could eat fish was the prototype of our resurrection body.[14]

Given these teachings, it stands to reason that those who die in Christ do, in fact, attend him upon death (cf. Acts 7: 59), but not in their final glorified state. Rather, they go to be with him in a strictly spiritual state – a provisional condition. When they return with Christ at the Second Coming, they will experience the change to that eternal state, being joined with their imperishable body. At that time, "…with a shout, with the voice of *the* archangel and with the trumpet of God…the dead in Christ will rise first" (1 Thessalonians 4: 16).

Those who are in Christ and remain alive here on earth when he returns will also experience change. No one will see Heaven in a perishable physical body, but believers will be transformed (1 Corinthians 15: 51). Each one will receive the kind of imperishable spiritual body Jesus knew at his resurrection allowing them to join him in the spiritual world along with those who have gone before.

---

[14] Piper, John, *Does My Soul Sleep After Death?*, https://www.desiringgod.org/ interviews/does-my-soul-sleep-after-death, accessed May 25, 2020.

Chapter 5
Difficult Bible Passages

Approaching Scripture

It would be disingenuous to suggest that every verse of God's Word is written with such plain and simple language that misunderstanding is not possible. There are many passages of Scripture that present honest interpretive challenges. This is due in part to the fact that figurative or symbolic language is not always completely straightforward, particularly when it is translated from its original language. This is one of the reasons there is such an assortment of doctrinal views on a variety of biblical topics.

Another cause of doctrinal diversity has been driven by the fact that people approach Scripture from a range of perspectives. Often, a student of the Bible will carry into his or her studies a variety of preconceptions that have been learned from others (ministers, teachers, etc.). This can interfere with one's objectivity, particularly where seemingly difficult passages are concerned.

Understanding God's Word requires honesty and humility – traits that are often too easily set aside when it comes to one's approach to Scripture. When a doctrinal disagreement occurs, biblical study might be undertaken to prove oneself right rather than seek the truth. In such a case, pride, rather than an honest search for truth, often serves as guide.

God did not provide the Bible so men could decide what it does or does not mean from a personal perspective (2 Peter 1: 20). The Bible was given so that humankind could learn what the apostles taught. Here are some basic rules, drawn from an earlier work entitled *One*

Bible...And Yet, So Many Beliefs, that will help keep the honest student of Scripture solidly grounded in apostolic instruction. The first general rule to remember when studying Holy Writ is:

1. Interpret only when it is necessary.[15]

Much of God's Word needs no interpretation since it is written in straightforward fashion. People spend far too much energy over-analyzing Scripture. Given God's unequaled capacity to communicate, it seems reasonable to believe he has provided a book that needs little interpretation. While the apostles wrote figuratively at times, and there are some passages that present challenges, much of the teaching in the epistles is uncomplicated. The words of the apostles provide considerable insight into the Kingdom of Heaven. Unlike Jesus' parables, where the lesson was often obscured from listeners who were spiritually naive, the apostles' teachings are generally very direct. The epistles were written to the general membership of the church body rather than an elite group of scholars and should be read with that in mind.

While interpretation is generally unnecessary, it cannot be entirely dismissed since, at times, the Bible demands it. For example, the parables require a certain level of interpretation. However, where interpretation is necessary, it is important to apply sound interpretive principles in a reasonable manner. When interpreting a passage of Scripture, it is important to consider the context, the original intent of the author or speaker, and how the words would have been understood by the audience at the time. Personal beliefs cannot lead the way in interpretation. This serves as a good lead-in to a second general rule of interpretation with respect to Scripture.

2. Be objective when applying interpretive principles.[16]

Objectivity can be difficult to achieve at times. If a person has viewed a passage of Scripture through a specific doctrinal lens for a considerable length of time, separation from that view becomes nearly impossible. For this reason, few people honestly revisit their doctrinal views. Most are confident that they are *right* in their understanding of

---

[15] Carlson, Steven A., *One Bible...And Yet, So Many Beliefs*, Guardian Publishing, LLC, Holt, MI, 2014, p. 31.
[16] Ibid, p. 32.

Scripture and no honest biblical study would dare interfere. When someone is entrenched in a doctrinal view that fails to harmonize with the fullness of God's Word, they will insist that a verse says what they believe it says. Other verses are then seen through that same doctrinal lens and forced to agree while honest interpretation is set aside. This leads to the third and final general rule of interpretation relative to scriptural instruction.

    3. Do not try to force Scripture to harmonize. It will do this on its own.[17]

From Genesis through Revelation the Bible is true and it is axiomatic that true statements cannot conflict. Despite the many voices claiming that biblical conflicts exist, Scripture will not contradict itself since it is Spirit-inspired from beginning to end. Therefore, biblical accord need not be forced. Where apparent conflicts arise, it is generally a matter of recognizing the different perspectives from which the authors are writing. If it is necessary to rewrite biblical text to affect harmonization with one's view of a passage of Scripture, it is safe to say that the person's view of the passage is flawed.

Difficult Biblical Passages

It is undeniable that, within the pages of Scripture, certain passages can be difficult to understand. In part, this is due to cultural differences between the first century and the modern age. Also, imprecise interpretation caused by language barriers can be a problem since certain words and phrases do not translate well, but these are not the only factors. The apostles, inspired by the Holy Spirit, were colorful writers. Consequently, there are times when biblical verbiage makes it challenging to fully grasp the author's or speaker's meaning.

> **It is undeniable that, within the pages of Scripture, certain passages can be difficult to understand.**

When a passage of Scripture seems difficult to understand, the proper response is to learn what the biblical landscape has to say generally about the subject in question. There are some challenging Bible passages over which people tend to argue. These include discussions about spiritual gifts (cf. 1 Corinthians 13: 8-13), election (cf. Ephesians 1: 3-6), apostasy (cf. Hebrews 5: 4-6), the role of women

---

[17] Ibid, p. 33.

in the church (cf. 1 Timothy 2: 15), baptism (cf. John 3: 5), and others where it is said that certain verses are a bit unclear in their teaching.

No passage of Scripture should be considered the single source of authority on any given doctrine. The Bible abounds with instruction on each of these topics. When the lesson from a verse of Scripture seems ambiguous, it is best to set it aside and consider what the balance of Scripture teaches on the subject. The difficult verse should then be weighed against those with less complicated wording to determine how *both* can be true. This should help to sustain biblical harmony so that doctrinal truth will not be compromised.

Handling Difficult Passages

It is one thing to recognize that challenging passages exist. It is another matter to deal with them effectively. It seems wise, then, to establish reasonable guidelines that, if followed, will help avoid developing erroneous teachings that fail to harmonize with the balance of Scripture.

In a passage where the doctrine under consideration is not a redemptive matter, a person should not lose sleep simply because he or she has failed to fully grasp the author's meaning. Still, that does not make it any less perplexing or the Bible student any less curious. This is where guidelines might prove to be helpful. When it comes to understanding a difficult text, the following three tests can help one avoid drawing conclusions that are well off the mark. Since people have drawn a multitude of conclusions from 1 Timothy 2: 15, it is used here as an example for applying these guidelines.

> But women will be saved through childbearing—if they continue in faith, love and holiness with propriety. (1 Timothy 2: 15, NIV)

It should be obvious why this is considered a difficult text. In English translations, knowing what Scripture teaches about salvation and the birthing process, this passage is illogical. A wise first step in addressing a verse like this is to read other translations that might offer different perspectives. Unfortunately, other English translations do not offer much help where this verse is concerned, although *The Amplified Bible*, *The Complete Jewish Bible*, and *The Living Bible* provide interesting perspectives that are worth reviewing.

No attempt will be made here to solve the mystery of this text, but this verse offers an excellent opportunity to reasonably apply interpretive principles in a way that helps to avoid misleading conclusions or false doctrines. Here are some guidelines, also taken from *One Bible...And Yet, So Many Beliefs*, that may help in this process.

    1. The meaning must be reasonable.[18]

This is a common-sense test. For instance, if an interpretation of the text can be ruled out quickly and sensibly, then rule it out. Since the remarks in this verse are specific to women, conclusions about the meaning of the verse should reflect that fact. Paul has much to say to the young Timothy about men elsewhere in his epistle, but not in this verse. Drawing conclusions about men in a verse where they are not discussed would be unreasonable.

    2. The meaning must fit the context of the passage.[19]

When studying a challenging biblical text, it is wise to pay attention to the topic under consideration by the author. This involves examining the immediate context (the verses before and after the text in question) as well as the general theme of the epistle. In this instance, Paul is instructing Timothy about the distinctive roles of men and women in a congregational setting and why those roles exist. Therefore, Paul's words in this verse about women and childbearing must be related to that topic in some fashion.

    3. The meaning must harmonize with the balance of Scripture.[20]

This is a critical point. Obscurity in any given passage of Scripture does not give license to develop a doctrine that clashes with the general and specific themes in God's Word. That is why it is always best to search for other passages where similar discussions are in view. In fact, other verses may offer additional insight into the passage that is difficult to understand on its own. At the very least, any conclusions one might draw from the text cannot contradict the whole of Scripture.

Scholars and laymen alike disagree about Paul's lesson in 1 Timothy 2: 15, and there is no question that the verse is an interpretive

---

[18] Ibid, p. 40.
[19] Ibid
[20] Ibid

challenge. Nonetheless, most agree on what he is not saying. The apostle is not suggesting that women attain eternal salvation by giving birth. This kind of conclusion finds no support anywhere in Scripture and overtly conflicts with biblical instruction about the path to eternal life (c.f. Matthew 28: 19-20; John 3: 3-5, 16; Acts 2: 21, 38; 3: 19; 4: 12; 16: 31; Romans 10: 13; Ephesians 2: 8). Therefore, childbirth (at least in the common physical sense) can be ruled out as means to attaining spiritual salvation.

Men have failed to come to agreement about the meaning of 1 Timothy 2: 15 over the past two millennia, and it is highly unlikely that they will unite around a single meaning for this verse soon. However, when addressing a difficult text like this, it is helpful to apply the three criteria mentioned above. This will not always lead to *the* clarification for which one might have hoped, but it can help avoid the pitfalls that can result in questionable conclusions.

Section 2

Proclamation to Spirits in Prison

Chapter 6
Alive in the Spirit
1 Peter 3:18

A Controversial Text

A key Bible passage from which men have developed the doctrine of Jesus' descent into Hell is found in the writings of the Apostle Peter. In recent times, men have relied heavily on 1 Peter 3: 18 – 4: 6 to support the claim that Jesus made such a journey, but that has not always been the case. Certain church fathers in the earliest days of the church believed Jesus took this spiritual journey. Ignatius of Antioch (AD 35-107) argued in favor of this doctrine as did others like Tertullian (AD 160-240) and Origen (AD 184-253). While these men appear to have had a shared view on *The Descensus*, they evidently drew much of their belief about Jesus' descent from extra-biblical sources such as *The First Book of Enoch* and by drawing inferences from certain Bible passages (cf. Matthew 12: 40; 27: 52-53; Acts 2: 27, 31; Ephesians 4: 9). 1 Peter was not the primary source from which they developed their views.

One thing that can be said about this passage, particularly with respect to the first two verses of the text, is that it can be categorized as one of those difficult passages mentioned in the previous section. While some believe the words provide a compelling portrait of Jesus descending into Hell, others are unconvinced. This chapter will focus primarily on the first verse of the text (v. 18), but to give some sense to this and the following chapters, here is the entire section that is under consideration.

> [18] For Christ also suffered for sins once for all *time, the* just for *the* unjust, so that He might bring us to God, having been put to death in the flesh, but made alive in the spirit; [19] in which He also went and made proclamation to the spirits in prison, [20] who once were disobedient when the patience of God kept waiting in the days of Noah, during the construction of the ark, in which a few, that is, eight persons, were brought safely through *the* water. [21] Corresponding to that, baptism now saves you—not the removal of dirt from the flesh, but an appeal to God for a good conscience—through the resurrection of Jesus Christ, [22] who is at the right hand of God, having gone into heaven, after angels and authorities and powers had been subjected to Him. **4** Therefore, since Christ has suffered in the flesh, arm yourselves also with the same purpose, because the one who has suffered in the flesh has ceased from sin, [2] so as to live the rest of the time in the flesh no longer for human lusts, but for the will of God. [3] For the time already past is sufficient *for you* to have carried out the desire of the Gentiles, having pursued a course of indecent behavior, lusts, drunkenness, carousing, drinking parties, and wanton idolatries. [4] In *all* this, they are surprised that you do not run with *them* in the same excesses of debauchery, and they slander *you*; [5] but they will give an account to Him who is ready to judge the living and the dead. [6] For the gospel has for this purpose been preached even to those who are dead, that though they are judged in the flesh as people, they may live in the spirit according to *the will of* God. (1 Peter 3: 18-4: 6)

The meaning of this passage has been debated throughout the church age, and it is unlikely that men will come to agreement in this life. The goal in this section is to reconsider some of the historical interpretations of the text and consider how Peter's words can be understood in a manner that harmonizes with the balance of Scripture.

Context

No verse of Scripture is an island. When determining the meaning of a passage of Scripture, the most important matter to be considered is the words of the text, but a close second is the context in which those words are spoken or written. The literary context entails: the subject matter of the chapter and book under consideration; the situation behind the writing; and the identity of those being addressed. Doctrinal conclusions must also be measured against the greater biblical landscape since the teaching found in one passage of Scripture does not outweigh, and cannot abrogate, teaching found elsewhere in God's Word.

Scholars generally agree about the overall focus of the content of Peter's first epistle, although there are assorted views when it comes to some of the details. It is, first and foremost, a book of inspiration with teaching about salvation through Christ's suffering, death, and resurrection leading the way. The audience is encouraged to value their salvation and recognize that God will watch over them even in difficult times. Whatever the circumstances, they should live their lives in submission to God. Experiencing suffering as a believer is not uncommon, but it is not reason to be discouraged.

Some Bible scholars have suggested that the book of 1 Peter is a written representation of a sermon the apostle spoke at a baptismal service. One author states that 1 Peter 3: 18-22, "…is a short gospel message preached at a baptismal service…"[21] Another writer comments, "A very interesting theory of the usage of the letter is that it was a letter intended to be read at a baptismal service with the purpose of strengthening the faith of the baptized as they find themselves living as exiles in an alien culture."[22]

Put to Death in the Flesh

In the few verses leading up to Peter's words about Jesus' suffering and death, reassurance is offered to those in his audience who were experiencing persecution from the outside world. They should not despair, according to Peter, since they were not suffering for doing evil, but for doing good. The kind of suffering they were experiencing could be worn as a badge of honor, since suffering for doing what is right is admirable (1 Peter 3: 14-17). Jesus is then offered as the perfect example of suffering for doing good.

When Jesus died on the cross, and subsequently rose again as a matter of conquering death, he died on behalf of all men as a substitute sacrifice for human sin, both past and future. Why would Christ die in man's place? The goal was simple. He did this "…so that He might bring us to God" (v. 18). Sin had erected a spiritually impenetrable

---

[21] Holdcroft, Mark, *Baptism*, https://www.sermoncentral.com/sermons/baptism-mark-holdcroft-sermon-on-baptism-59607, accessed May 28, 2020.

[22] Jensen, Richard, *Commentary on 1 Peter 1: 3-9*, http://www.workingpreacher.org/preaching.aspx?commentary_id=57, accessed May 28, 2020.

barrier between God and men; at least, it was impenetrable from man's perspective. God chose to breach the barrier himself by paying the necessary cost. As a matter of salvation, Jesus was submissively put to death physically for righteousness' sake, "*the* just for *the* unjust" (v. 18).

The phrase, "in the flesh" (v. 18), implies that there was something special about the life of Christ relative to the manner of his death. After all, what other way is there for men to die? It would be foolish to suggest that men die in any other fashion (notwithstanding the spiritual death of those who reject Christ), so why would Peter specifically refer to Jesus' crucifixion as a death "in the flesh?"

Every human being dies a physical death since flesh is man's nature. However, flesh was not Jesus' nature. He had to *assume* a fleshly existence (cf. John 1: 14; 1 Timothy 3: 16; 1 John 4: 2; 2 John 1: 7) to accomplish his purpose. That is what made physical death for Christ so exceptional. He is the one person who has died in human history for whom a bodily death was not mandated. Nevertheless, he *chose* to assume a body of flesh and die as other men die.

There is no reason to believe that the physical death Jesus suffered was different from the kind of physical death all men experience. Therefore, it makes sense that it involved separation of body and spirit just like other men (cf. Genesis 35: 18; Luke 23: 46). No Scripture contradicts this principle, and those who have a reasonable understanding of God's Word tend to agree on this tenet. While certain portions of this section of Scripture are deemed challenging and have resulted in considerable division among believers, there is general agreement where the meaning of this statement about Jesus' death is concerned.

Made Alive in the Spirit

Peter's statement that Jesus was "...put to death in the flesh," is immediately followed by his recognition that he was "...made alive in the spirit" (v. 18). It is the apostle's use of this expression that has caused some confusion and led to different perspectives where this section of Scripture is concerned.

There are primarily two views about the meaning behind these words. Many believe that this is simply Peter recognizing the fact of Jesus' resurrection from the dead. This verse, it is said, offers a concise synopsis of the gospel message (the death and resurrection of Christ). Others insist that these words offer insight into the unseen spiritual world and the activities of Jesus' spirit while his physical body lay lifeless. The following paragraphs may seem overwhelming, given the nature of the topic and the depth of the Greek grammar involved in this section, but the basic question is whether Peter's words in the text (v. 18) point to Jesus' *physical resurrection* or his *spiritual activities prior to his resurrection.*

The belief that Peter's words provide a glimpse into the unseen world is grounded partly in the words of the ensuing verse with the statement, "...in which also He went and made proclamation to the spirits in prison" (v. 19). According to this view, the phrase "...in the spirit" (v. 18) serves as the predicate for the activity described in the next verse. The teaching is that when Jesus died, his spirit, separated from his body, journeyed to a place where certain spirits were being held in a spiritual prison. There he either preached the gospel or offered some other statement/proclamation to those beings who were imprisoned.

The Greek terminology that is translated into the English phrase "...made alive in the spirit" is *zōopoiētheis de tō pneumati*, which the *Holy Bible Literal Version* renders "...but was given life in *the* Spirit." The KJV uses the phrase "...quickened by the Spirit." To *quicken* is to *bring to life*, or *to revive*. Some form of the Greek word *zōopoieō* appears eleven times in the New Testament. In each case, whether figuratively or literally, it speaks of *bringing to life* or, more commonly, *restoring life* to that which is dead. The following verses from John and Romans expressly connect *zōopoieō* with restoring life to that which is dead. These renderings are from *The Bible in Basic English*, which offers a true sense of the meaning of this word.

> In the same way, as the Father gives life (zōopoiē) to the dead, even so the Son gives life (zōopoiē) to those to whom He is pleased to give it. (John 5: 21, TBBE)

> (As it is said in the holy Writings, I have made you a father of a number of nations) before him whom he had faith, that is, God, who gives life (zōopoiountos) to the dead, and to whom the things which are not are as if they were. (Romans 4: 17, TBBE)

> But if the Spirit of him who made Jesus come again from the dead is in you, he who made Christ Jesus come again from the dead will in the same way, through the Spirit which is in you, give life (zōopoiēsēi) to your bodies which now are under the power of death. (Romans 8: 11, TBBE)

The meaning of the phrase, "...in the spirit" is key when unpacking the apostle's message, since what one believes about Jesus being "made alive," whether physically or spiritually, depends largely on the sense in which the term *spirit* is understood. That discussion specifically involves a look at Peter's use of the phrase *tō pneumati* which is rendered variously in assorted English translations. The NASV offers the translation "in the spirit."

The KJV translators have capitalized *Spirit* in this instance, indicating that they believed Jesus' bodily resurrection was in view and it was the Holy Spirit who facilitated that resurrection. This interpretation finds some support in the text since *tō* (the) precedes *pneumati*. This is often the case when the Holy Spirit is in view. The idea presented in the KJV translation suggests that Jesus was brought back to life *by the* (tō) Holy Spirit following his suffering and death. This would be in keeping with the passive tense of *zōopoiētheis* indicating that Jesus had a passive role in his resurrection. The combination of the Spirit's involvement and Jesus' passivity in the resurrection finds considerable support in the pages of Scripture (cf. Acts 2: 24; 3: 15; Romans 1: 4; 8: 11; 2 Corinthians 4: 14; 15: 4; Galatians 1: 1; 1 Thessalonians 1: 10; Hebrews 13: 20).

Those who believe that these verses speak of Jesus' activity in the spiritual world behind the tomb generally prefer the translation *in the* (tō) spirit, believing it depicts Jesus leaving his physical body behind while being made alive *in a strictly spiritual state in the spiritual world*. The interpretive preference of *tō*, in this case, is evidently based largely on doctrinal preference. For this reason, this section of this verse has been interpreted as follows by various translators.

> Christ was put to death as a human, but made alive by the Spirit. (Common English Bible)

> In his physical form he was killed, but he was made alive by the Spirit. (Easy to Read Version)

> and was put to death concerning the flesh, but was quickened by the spirit. (1599 Geneva Bible)

> He was put to death physically, but made alive spiritually, (Good News Translation)

> He was put to death in a mortal body but was brought to life by the Spirit (International Standard Version)

He went through it all—was put to death and then made alive—to bring us to God. (The Message)

Though He died in the flesh, He was made alive again through the Spirit. (The Voice)

These numerous English renderings indicate that the meaning of *tō pneumati* is open to interpretation. There is no single, clean translation for this expression. It does not translate well into English, which makes it difficult to come to agreement about the meaning of the apostle's words. A verbatim translation, according to Scripture4All Interlinear Bible, would read "Being-(caused to) die indeed to-flesh being made-alive to-the spirit."

An important point when considering the meaning of the expression *tō pneumati* in this context is that the conjunction translated into English as "but" (Gr. *de*) appears to contrast the life Jesus received (Gr. *zōopoiētheis*) against the death (Gr. *thanatōtheis*) he experienced. This suggests that the life mentioned here points to the resurrection since it is physical life rather than spiritual life that is the antithesis of physical death.

When the fullness of Scripture is considered, it becomes evident that the verbiage *tō pneumati* (v. 18) need not be seen as the single determinant for the meaning of the expression "made alive" since Holy Writ speaks abundantly to this topic. From Acts through Revelation, Jesus' death is mentioned more than five dozen times, and it is discussed almost exclusively in the context of his physical resurrection, which is generally mentioned in the same verse. Exceptions to this can be found in 1 Corinthians where Paul's focus is on those who crucified Christ (cf. 1 Corinthians 1: 23; 2: 8) and a verse where Paul professes his intent "…to know nothing among you except Jesus Christ, and Him crucified" (1 Corinthians 2: 2). Later chapters in 1 Corinthians dwell heavily on Jesus' resurrection.

Where the Apostle Peter is concerned, there is no occasion in Scripture where he addresses Christ's death outside the immediate context of his resurrection. Without exception, whether on the day of Pentecost (Acts 2: 23-24, 31-32), in his sermon at the portico of Solomon (Acts 3: 14-15), before the Israelite elders (Acts 4: 10), in the presence of the high priest and Sadducees (Acts 5: 30), or as he met with Cornelius and other Gentiles in Caesarea (Acts 10: 39-41), Peter consistently blends his comments about the death and resurrection of Christ, portraying them as inseparable.

The phrase "...put to death in the flesh" (v. 18) represents the apostle's third reference to Jesus' death in the epistle. On those earlier occasions (1 Peter 1: 3, 21), this same pattern is present. In each verse, Jesus' death and resurrection are bound together. If Peter's words "...made alive in the spirit" are not intended to depict Jesus rising physically from the tomb, it represents an uncharacteristic departure from his historically consistent approach when discussing Jesus' death.

Peter's practice of declaring Jesus' death and resurrection in tandem is firmly established in the pages of Scripture. It is highly unlikely that 1 Peter 3: 18 is the single example of the apostle forsaking that pattern, especially when the words "put to death in the flesh, but made alive in the spirit" seem to support it. This would require not only accepting that Peter abandoned his tradition of intimately connecting Jesus' death and resurrection, but that he significantly altered course, taking his readers on a nebulous journey into the unseen world beyond the grave.

In his first letter to the Corinthians, Paul wrote significantly concerning Jesus' resurrection. In fact, the fifteenth chapter of that letter is devoted fully to teaching about resurrection. In that soliloquy, the question is raised hypothetically by Paul himself about the nature of a resurrected body (1 Corinthians 15: 35). The apostle answers the question for his readers, explaining that a resurrected body, at least one suited for the spiritual world, is a body with spiritual characteristics.

In his letter to the church in Rome, Paul portrays Adam as "...a pattern of the one to come" (Romans 5: 14), who is Jesus. The idea is that Adam is the type and Jesus is the antitype. In other words, the two can be considered mirror images of one another. The apostle employs this analogy when writing to the Corinthians about resurrection, explaining that death came through Adam while (spiritual) life comes through Christ (1 Corinthians 15: 22).

Paul continues, offering a contrast between what he calls the natural human body and a resurrected spiritual body (1 Corinthians 15: 44). In that vein, he distinguishes between the first Adam and the last Adam (Jesus). Citing Genesis 2: 7, the apostle explains that "The first MAN, Adam, BECAME A LIVING SOUL" (1 Corinthians 15: 45, NASV 1995 Edition). However, he says of Jesus, "The last Adam *became* a life-giving spirit" (1 Corinthians 15: 45, NASV 1995 Edition).

These words about Jesus are written in the context of Paul's treatise on resurrection. Consequently, Bible scholars recognize that the phrase "*became* a life-giving spirit" is not intended to direct anyone to the time Jesus' body lay in the tomb, but to his resurrection from the tomb. Peter's teaching that Jesus was "…made alive in the spirit" seems to echo the Apostle Paul's words to the Corinthians. In fact, the Greek terminology in these two instances is essentially identical (*zōopoiētheis de tō pneumati* vs *pneuma zōopoioun*), with Peter emphasizing the *fact* of the resurrection while Paul offers a more descriptive portrait of Jesus' post-resurrection *state*. It stands to reason, then, that 1 Peter 3: 18 also depicts the death and resurrection of Christ.

When the content and context of Peter's words are fully and honestly considered, his statement is easily recognized as a summation of the same gospel message that is recorded throughout the New Testament. It is the same gospel message Peter has in view every time he mentions Jesus' death. The following English translations fittingly treat 1 Peter 3: 18 as a portrait of the death and resurrection of Christ.

> Christ himself suffered for sins once [*or* once for all; only his suffering has the power to redeem others]. He was not guilty, but he suffered for those who are guilty […the righteous for the unrighteous] to bring you to God. His body was killed [He was put to death in the flesh/body], but he was made alive in the spirit [*or* Spirit; at his resurrection in a glorified body]. (Expanded Bible)

> Christ also suffered once for sins. The one who did what is right suffered for those who don't do right. He suffered to bring you to God. His body was put to death. But the Holy Spirit brought him back to life. (New International Reader's Version).

The intent of this passage is to encourage the believers to look beyond their current suffering (vv. 14-17). With that theme in mind, Peter forges ahead (v. 18), beginning with the word "For" (Gr. *hoti*), which indicates that the message of this verse is intended to supplement those words of encouragement. Jesus suffered and died, but the long game was his glorious resurrection and ascension along with the eventual resurrection of those who place their faith in him.

Chapter 7
Going and Proclaiming
1 Peter 3:19-20

In Which

If 1 Peter 3: 18 can be considered challenging, it represents but a molehill when measured against the mountainous terrain of the next verse. Beginning with the prepositional phrase "in which" (Gr. *en hō*), 1 Peter 3: 19 speaks to some activity on Jesus' part and the activity begins with Jesus *going* (Gr. *poreutheis*) somewhere. The phrase "in which" is presumed by most to apply to Jesus' state of being at the time, thus, the word "which" requires an antecedent and must refer to something in the verse prior.

Jesus was "...alive in the spirit." That is his state of being that was previously established (v. 18). Therefore, many identify "spirit" as the appropriate antecedent. Consequently, Jesus' activities (v. 19), it is argued, must be seen in that vein. In other words, Jesus performed these activities *in a spiritual state*. Although, the construction of the text suggests that this narrow view is not necessary.

Assorted English translations offer varying interpretations for *en hō*, suggesting that its use here is more general. For instance, the NIV 1984 Edition employs the phrase "...through whom," the NIV 2011 Edition uses the expression "...after being made alive," the NIRV rendering is

"...after that," the NLT translates using the simple word "...so," and the CEV uses the term "...then." One popular commentary observes:

> As to the words of the passage: **through whom** need not necessarily mean 'through the spirit' but may be no more than a general resumptive expression 'and so' or 'in the course of which' (cf. on 1: 6).[23]

This seems to be a reasonable explanation for *en hō* in this setting. The term portrays the activity described here (v. 19) as following the resurrection (v. 18). If "...alive in the spirit" depicts Jesus' resurrected state, which aligns with Paul's recognition that Jesus "...*became* a life-giving spirit" at the time of his resurrection (1 Corinthians 15: 45), then it is his resurrected state that is in view with the term *en hō*. Norman Ericson is cognizant of this, stating:

> This journey of Christ took place after the resurrection rather than between his death and resurrection, since the description follows the resurrection in verse 18, and the relative clause "in which" (en ho) refers either to his resurrected spiritual state, or "at that time," that is, after his death and resurrection.[24]

William Dalton has written two of the more comprehensive works on this passage of Scripture. Entitled *Christ's Proclamation to the Spirits – A Study of 1 Peter 3:18-4:6*, his first edition was published in 1965 with a second edition in 1989. Some of his conclusions are open to debate, but that can be said of any conclusions derived from this passage. Still, he does see verse eighteen as a depiction of Christ's death and resurrection. In that vein, like Norman Ericson, he recognizes that the events of verse nineteen take place in Jesus' post-resurrection state.

> Once it is admitted, in keeping with New Testament usage, that ζωοποιηθεὶς πνεύματι refers to Christ's bodily resurrection, then the "going" and the "proclaiming" of Christ should be taken as aspects of his activity after the resurrection.[25]

---

[23] Bruce, F. F., General Editor, The New International Bible Commentary, Zondervan, Grand Rapids, 1979, p. 1559
[24] Ericson, Norman R., Spirits in Prison, https://www.biblestudytools.com/dictionaries/bakers-evangelical-dictionary/spirits-in-prison.html, accessed June 4, 2020.
[25] Dalton, William, *Christ's Proclamation to the Spirits – A Study of 1 Peter 3:18-4:6*, Catholic Theological College, Melbourne, 1989, p. 24.

Dalton recognizes that the only other place in Scripture where this specific Greek wording appears (1 Corinthians 15: 45), it serves as an incontrovertible reference to Jesus' resurrection – a fact that is accepted by scholars and laymen of all doctrinal persuasions. To this can be added the fact that *zōopoieō* is generally used to depict restoration of life to that which is dead. Consequently, insisting that it holds a different, highly questionable meaning in Peter's epistle represents a poor exegetical approach to the text.

The belief that Jesus' spirit journeyed to Hell as his body lay lifeless has been front and center for centuries, which makes it difficult for many to question that teaching. Nevertheless, if "...made alive in the spirit" speaks to Jesus' resurrection, which is in keeping with comparable Greek verbiage in the balance of Scripture, the activities described in the next verse would logically follow his resurrection.

Moving deeper into the text, serious questions arise. According to Peter, Jesus did something while he was *alive in the spirit* (resurrected). The apostle states that, having been "[18]...made alive in the spirit, ...[19]He also went and made proclamation to the spirits in prison." The questions that jump off the page are:

1. Where did Jesus go?
2. What proclamation did he make?
3. Who are the spirits to whom Jesus made a proclamation?
4. To what prison is the apostle referring?

Having Gone

Even though the text has mystified scholars for two millennia, Peter offers his words rather casually. There seems to be an assumption that his readers would fully appreciate the nature of Jesus' *going*, the message in his proclamation, and the identities of the spirits and the prison.

Peter was not personally familiar with everyone who would read his letter. It was written "To those who reside as strangers, scattered throughout Pontus, Galatia, Cappadocia, Asia, and Bithynia, who are chosen" (1 Peter 1: 1). That is a wide audience, and the letter would have been well-circulated among the churches of Asia Minor. It would have been read or heard by tens of thousands of believers even in the first century, to say nothing of the countless individuals who have read these words over the ages.

Since Peter seemingly anticipated that such a diverse audience would, even without a detailed explanation, recognize the nature of Jesus' *going* and *proclaiming* as well as the identity of the *spirits* (v. 19), the meaning must have been evident to them. Consequently, it must involve something that was either common knowledge among the believers of the first century or is revealed within the immediate text. It is doubtful that the apostle intended to leave everyone scratching their heads at a time when he was attempting to offer words of encouragement.

Addressing the first question (above) concerning Jesus' destination, some have quickly jumped to the conclusion that Jesus *journeyed to the prison where the spirits reside*. That presumption is based primarily on the notion that the activity described here (v. 19) takes place between Jesus' death and resurrection. However, if "...put to death in the flesh, but made alive in the spirit" (v. 18) depicts the death and resurrection of Christ, it is difficult to see how the events of the ensuing verse might reflect Jesus' days in the tomb. The flow of the narrative suggests that these events follow the resurrection.

If Jesus' *going* and *proclaiming* (v. 19) follow the resurrection, which appears to be the case, that narrows the possibilities considerably. Jesus spent forty days on earth after his resurrection, and Scripture does not provide much information about his activities during that time. He met with the disciples and others several times but, beyond that, Scripture is silent. It is unlikely that Peter would have directed the believers' attention to a journey about which the balance of Scripture provides no information.

Jesus' ascension is the one event with which all believers would have been familiar since it is critical to the gospel message. In the immediate context, a mere three verses later (v. 22), *poreutheis* points unmistakably to the ascension, Jesus *having gone* to Heaven. It is reasonable to believe that, since they are proximate in the text, *poreutheis* would carry the same meaning each time (vv. 19 & 22), the second verse serving to establish/confirm the identity of the *going* mentioned earlier in the narrative. This explains why Peter felt confident that his readers would understand. On this point, Dalton makes the following observation.

When one asks what "going" of Christ is found in the traditional teaching of the New Testament, the obvious reply indicates the ascension. In fact, the same term used in 3:22 would lead us to expect in 3:19 the same event.[26]

The most reasonable solution is that *poreutheis* identifies the same *going* (Jesus' ascension) in both verses of the narrative. This is the single post-resurrection journey that would need no explanation since all Christians were and are familiar with Jesus' ascension.

The nature of Jesus' "...proclamation to the spirits in prison" (v. 19) has not yet been addressed. It is difficult to know the character of that message without delving into the balance of the narrative, so this will be considered a little later. In the meantime, exactly who are these mysterious spirits?

The Spirits

While Jesus' *going* might be associated with his ascension, the nature of his proclamation and the identity of the spirits to whom he made his proclamation remain a mystery for most modern theologians; but mystery was not Peter's intent. His objective was to offer encouragement and inspiration. On the heels of his remarks about *going* and *proclaiming*, he has provided for his readers the identity of the spirits in prison in the ensuing verse. They were, according to the apostle, those:

> ...who once were disobedient when the patience of God kept waiting in the days of Noah, during the construction of the ark, in which a few, that is, eight persons, were brought safely through *the* water. (1 Peter 3: 20)

These words seemingly address the question: *Who are the spirits?* They are Noah's peers – those who died in the flood. Yet even this straightforward apostolic explanation has failed to satisfy many who insist that Peter's words are open to a measure of interpretation. In order to address what some see as an opportunity for innovative analysis, a look into the time of the flood and the specific nature of Noah's contemporaries is necessary.

---

[26] Dalton, William, *Christ's Proclamation to the Spirits – A Study of 1 Peter 3:18-4:6*, Catholic Theological College, Melbourne, 1989, p. 27.

* * *

> ¹Now it came about, when mankind began to multiply on the face of the land, and daughters were born to them, ² that the sons of God saw that the daughters of mankind were beautiful; and they took wives for themselves, whomever they chose. ³ Then the LORD said, "My Spirit will not remain with man forever, because he is also flesh; nevertheless his days shall be 120 years." ⁴ The Nephilim were on the earth in those days, and also afterward, when the sons of God came in to the daughters of mankind, and they bore children to them. Those were the mighty men who *were* of old, men of renown. ⁵ Then the LORD saw that the wickedness of mankind was great on the earth, and that every intent of the thoughts of their hearts was only evil continually. ⁶ So the LORD was sorry that He had made mankind on the earth, and He was grieved in His heart. ⁷ Then the LORD said, "I will wipe out mankind whom I have created from the face of the land; mankind, and animals as well, and crawling things, and the birds of the sky. For I am sorry that I have made them." ⁸ But Noah found favor in the eyes of the LORD. (Genesis 6: 1-8)

Prior to the flood, humankind spiraled away from God into a depraved state of evil. Mankind's condition deteriorated to the point that God decided to destroy the being he had created in his own image. Although, even with all the decadence that had ravaged humanity, one man stood out. God saw that Noah was a righteous man.

The "spirits in prison" in the narrative of 1 Peter are recognized as the unfaithful of Noah's day. That seems uncomplicated, but some believe it is more complex than simply identifying these spirits as Noah's contemporaries. The expression "sons of God" that appears in the Genesis account (Genesis 6: 2, 4) has been used to read something more elaborate into Peter's words.

The topic of fallen angels is raised in the New Testament by both Peter and Jude. They are described as "…angels who did not keep their own domain but abandoned their proper dwelling place" (Jude 1: 6). Where the days prior to the flood are concerned, some believe that the term "sons of God" refers to fallen angels (those mentioned by Jude) who saw the women God had created and, desiring them, left the spiritual world and married women of earth (Genesis 6: 2). The Nephilim, it is said, represent the offspring of these unholy alliances (Genesis 6: 4). It is argued that, rather than all of Noah's peers, it is these *fallen angels* whom Peter identifies as "spirits in prison."

The teaching is further advanced with the claim by some that the term for *spirits* (Gr. *pneumasin*) in 1 Peter 3: 19 points specifically to other-worldly beings such as unclean spirits or demons. That is a difficult case to make since comparable wording is used elsewhere to describe "...the spirits of *the* righteous" (Hebrews 12: 23). In the New Testament, when unclean or evil spirits are in view, they are consistently identified in the narrative as either demons (Gr. *daimonion*), evil (Gr. *ponêron*), or unclean (Gr. *akatharta*). There is no such designation in the current text. To this can be added the fact that, in this context, numerous Greek scholars recognize *pneumasin* as a reference to the departed spirits of human beings.

The Bible offers no indication that angels are capable of procreation or *self-transforming* into human bodies. When asked by the Sadducees about relationships in the spiritual world, Jesus spoke plainly to this topic, explaining, "...in the resurrection they neither marry nor are given in marriage, but are like angels in heaven" (Matthew 22: 30). While some are tempted to link the words of Jude about fallen angels with the events in Genesis, Scripture does not make that connection. It has been suggested by others that fallen angels may have *possessed* men to have sexual relations with the women of earth, but nothing in God's Word leads to that conclusion.

The phrase "sons of God" (Heb. *bni e·aleim*) is used three times in the book of Job where it points to angelic beings (Job 1: 6; 2: 1; 38: 7). The prophet Hosea employs comparable wording to depict faithful Israelites whom he calls, "...sons of the living God" (Hosea 1: 10). In the Old Testament, similar use can be seen in Deuteronomy 14: 1 and Psalm 82: 6. Comparable wording (albeit, in Greek) is found in a discussion between Jesus and some Sadducees as he offered instruction about what Heaven would be like for resurrected believers, stating, "...they are like angels, and are sons of God" (Luke 20: 36). In that setting, much like Jesus' comments from Matthew, the term identifies departed believers as their state of being is likened to that of angels. Other places in the New Testament, the writers use the term *sons of God* to depict the faithful who are still living (Romans 8: 14, 19; 9: 26; Galatians 3: 26; 4: 6).

These examples demonstrate biblical flexibility in the use of this terminology. Still, it seems a considerable stretch to identify those in the Genesis account as fallen angels. While comparable wording is used to identify heavenly angels who have not fallen from grace or humans (living or dead) who have remained faithful, nowhere else in Scripture do these words identify fallen angels.

The prospect of identifying *sons of God* as fallen angels faces an additional biblical hurdle, and it is found in the book of Numbers. When the Israelites originally reached the promised land, Moses sent certain men to scout the land and report back (Numbers 13: 1-24). Upon their return, they told Moses that the land was bountiful, but at least some of the people were of enormous size and seemed as giants to them. Among these giants were the Nephilim (Numbers 13: 33). If the Nephilim who lived prior to the flood died in the flood, how is it that they appear in the book of Numbers hundreds of years later?

When the men Moses had sent offered their report, they described the Nephilim as large men, stating, "…we were like grasshoppers in our own sight" (Numbers 13: 33). Three of the Nephilim who are named specifically (Numbers 13: 22) were the sons of a man named Anak (Numbers 13: 33) who, in turn, was the son of a man by the name of Arba (Joshua 15: 13). If the Nephilim were descended from fallen angels, Arba would necessarily be either a Nephilim or a fallen angel and Anak would necessarily have been Nephilim. Nothing in the text suggests that Arba was Nephilim or a fallen angel, only that Anak's sons were among the Nephilim. It seems, then, that these two were mere mortals, and the Nephilim were not descendants of fallen angels.

Scripture does not provide insight into the Nephilim or the reason for their enormous size (evidently comparable to the Philistine known as Goliath), but there is no hint that they were more than human. In fact, the word Nephilim is a transliteration of the Hebrew term meaning *distinguished ones,* or *giants* (Heb. *e·nphlim*) and the children born to them are called *mortals of renown* (Heb. *anshi e·shim*). The term *anshi* appears more than one hundred times in the Old Testament, consistently referring to *mortal men.* To this can be added the fact that it was specifically *men of flesh*, rather than fallen angels, with whom God was angry (Genesis 6: 3). While some wish to introduce fallen angels into the text in 1 Peter based on this narrative from Genesis, God's Word fails to support that conclusion.

Who were the *sons of God* in Genesis? If not fallen angels, the term must refer to human beings. Many scholars rightly apply the term to the pious sons of Seth, of whom Noah was a descendant, whose line was faithful to God for a time. This is in keeping with the use of this terminology elsewhere in God's Word.

As discussed early in this work, reading Scripture in context is vital. Since the faithfulness of Seth's family (Genesis 4: 24-5: 32) is the context in which the term "sons of God" is used (Genesis 6: 2, 4), the connection with that lineage is sewn into the fabric of the narrative. As this line of godly men began to intermarry with the seed of the unfaithful, the results were catastrophic. It was the union of the sons of God (the faithful line of Seth) and the daughters of men (the unfaithful) that led humankind away from God.

* * *

Returning to 1 Peter, in the phrase, "spirits in prison" (v. 19), the editors of the NASV 1995 Edition have inserted *now* into the text so that it reads, "spirits *now* in prison." The word is not found in original Greek manuscripts, which is why it is italicized in the translation. The implication from this addition is that the spirits mentioned here were in prison at the time of Peter's writing but were not in prison at the time Jesus, being in the spirit, made his proclamation. This approach to the apostle's words relies on an understanding of the text that was developed in the early fifth century.

In the early church, as the debate grew concerning post-mortem conversion and the meaning of 1 Peter 3: 18-20, a bishop named Augustine (AD 354-430) was challenged to address the text. Based on Peter's reference to the time of Noah (v. 20), he concluded that Jesus' proclamation was made during the days of Noah prior to the flood. The solution was that Jesus, in spirit (v. 18), spoke through Noah to the wicked of that day. While neither the Genesis narrative nor the narrative of 1 Peter specifically states that Noah proclaimed anything, Peter later wrote of Noah's preaching (2 Peter 2: 5). Augustine also believed that the simple act of building the ark would have served as proclamation, or witness, to the people of Noah's time (Genesis 6: 9-16).

Augustine's interpretation of the text has become widely accepted among modern Protestantism. One reason for this favorable response is that his explanation does not conflict doctrinally with the balance of Scripture. This does not mean it is the correct interpretation of the text, but it does provide a sense of reasonableness, which is vital when addressing a difficult passage.

As he developed his position on 1 Peter 3: 18-20, Augustine leaned heavily on a passage from the first chapter of Peter's letter where the apostle depicts Christ's spirit speaking through the prophets of old (1 Peter 1: 10-12). He then reasoned that this must be what Peter had in view when he wrote/spoke of Jesus making a proclamation to spirits in prison.

While Augustine was surely well-intentioned, this explanation seems forced. It is not what one would naturally glean from reading the text since the apostle does not say that Jesus' spirit spoke *through Noah* to the spirits in prison. Peter would have to presume that his audience would effortlessly make the connection with the earlier passage. That is a weak argument given the fact that the church fathers failed to recognize that relationship in the first four hundred years of church writings. In fact, it purportedly took Augustine considerable deliberation to draw his conclusions, which he considered frail. He wrote the following when presenting his resolution to the text.

> *To My Lord Evodius Most Blessed, My Brother and Partner in the Episcopal Office, Augustine Sends Greeting in the Lord.*
>
> The question which you have proposed to me from the epistle of the Apostle Peter is one which, as I think you are aware, is wont to perplex me most seriously, namely, how the words which you have quoted are to be understood on the supposition that they were spoken concerning Hell? I therefore refer this question back to yourself, that if either you yourself be able, or can find any other person who is able to do so, you may remove and terminate my perplexities on the subject. If the Lord grant to me ability to understand the words before you do, and it be in my power to impart what I receive from Him to you, I will not withhold it from a friend so truly loved. In the meantime, I will communicate to you the things in the passage which occasion difficulty to me, that, keeping in view these remarks on the words of the apostle, you may either exercise your own thoughts on them, or consult any one whom you find competent to pronounce an opinion.[27]

Augustine indicated that if his friend, Evodius, could derive a more reasoned solution, he was open to listening, suggesting that he was not completely comfortable with his own explanation. Augustine's words, along with the fact that no one in the first four centuries of the church understood that Peter was writing of Jesus speaking *through* Noah, make it difficult to imagine that this was how Peter's immediate audience would have understood these words in the first century.

---

[27] CHURCH FATHERS: Letter 164 (St. Augustine) (newadvent.org), accessed February 5, 2021.

It is curious that, although many rely heavily on his uncertain explanation of 1 Peter 3: 19-20 to refute the claim of Jesus' descent into Hell, Augustine never denied that the Lord made such a journey. In fact, he fully believed Jesus descended into Hell. In the very letter where he offered his position on this passage of Scripture, he mused, "Who, therefore, except an infidel, will deny that Christ was in Hell?"[28] To this he added, "It is established beyond question that the Lord, after He had been put to death in the flesh, 'descended into Hell.'"[29] Augustine's elucidation on 1 Peter was meant to oppose the doctrine of post mortem conversion, since some were claiming that Jesus *preached the gospel* to the spirits, offering salvation to those who had already passed from this life. It seems he would consider as infidels those who attempt to use his explanation of the text to deny *The Descensus*.

Peter invokes the antediluvians (those people who lived prior to, or at the time of, the flood) in his message of encouragement, but for what purpose? What lesson was he trying to convey in a session centered on uplifting his readers? What was the nature of Jesus' proclamation that it would apply specifically to this set of spirits? These are puzzling questions and will be addressed in full. However, consideration will first be given to the prison mentioned in the text.

The Prison

Just as one's transformation from a natural physical body to an eternal spiritual body is mysterious (1 Corinthians 15: 51), so the configuration of the unseen world is unknowable from this side of the grave (1 Corinthians 2: 9). Scripture offers some figurative imagery to describe places like Heaven (cf. John 14: 2) and Hell (cf. Mark 9: 43), but it is impossible to visualize spiritual domains from a human perspective.

The Apostle Peter uses a word that is intended as a depiction of a domain found in the spiritual world. The term *prison* (Gr. *phulakē*) is utilized in connection with the imprisonments of John the Baptist (Matthew 14: 3), Peter (Acts 12: 5), Paul (Acts 16: 19-23), and others. In Peter's first epistle and in Revelation, it is associated with a setting in the unseen world (1 Peter 3: 19; Revelation 18: 2).

---

[28] Ibid
[29] Ibid

Some have speculated that *prison* points to Hell in this context, but that position seems discordant with biblical instruction about this spiritual domain. The fiery Hell is a place of punishment for those whom God, in the final judgment, deems to have been unfaithful. It is not a waiting room for those who have passed from this life. Others have reasoned that the prison of which Peter wrote is Tartarus, mentioned by the apostle in his second epistle (2 Peter 2: 4), and the spirits were fallen angels – specifically the fallen angels of Noah's time – who were awaiting their judgment. However, that idea has been considered and dismissed.

It has further been theorized that "the spirits" in Peter's message might refer to those antediluvians who, when the rains came, called out to God, repenting of their sins. The supposition is that, in their spiritually imprisoned state, Jesus proclaimed to them the gospel message, offering an opportunity for salvation. This proposition is saddled with two primary difficulties. First, there is no record of repentance by those who died in the flood. If they did cry out to God as the rain began to fall, he surely considered their repentance insincere, knowing their evil ways. Their hearts had been revealed over many decades as Noah witnessed to them. Second, preaching the gospel message and offering eternal life to those who have already passed from this life conflicts with biblical teaching about the path to salvation. It is difficult to see why these, arguably the most scandalous and stubborn of sinners, would be the exception to those biblical principles.

According to Peter, the spirits of Noah's contemporaries were imprisoned in the spiritual world. Their eternal fortune was sealed when God closed the doors of the ark and the waters rained down from the heavens. They were now awaiting the final judgment as is the case with all who have been unfaithful to God, but where were they waiting?

When Jesus related to his disciples the story about the rich man and Lazarus, he painted a picture of the rich man in Hádes after his death where he was in torment (Luke 16: 22-23). The term Hádes, at times, serves as a portrait of death, or the grave. However, where the rich man is concerned, it is presented as a spiritual place of waiting where this man was fully cognizant of his situation and his condemnation.

Parables are not given to make doctrinal statements, but there is additional biblical support behind the idea that Hádes is a waiting place for the unfaithful. The Old Testament equivalent of the Greek word Hádes is the Hebrew word She'ol. While it commonly speaks of death, or the grave, there are occasions when it specifically describes a spiritual place for the wicked (cf. Psalm 9: 17; 55: 15; Ezekiel 32: 21) where self-awareness is very much a part of the picture. The Apostle John, in his apocalyptic vision, explains that all in Hádes, the spiritual waiting place for the lost, will eventually be "...thrown into the lake of fire" (Revelation 20: 14).

The antediluvians were disobedient. Prior to the flood, humanity had reached the point where "...the LORD saw that the wickedness of mankind was great on the earth, and that every intent of the thoughts of their hearts was only evil continually" (Genesis 6: 5). If Hádes is the unseen domain where the spirits of the unfaithful are preserved for judgment, a reasonable conclusion is that this is where the souls of these individuals remain even today. It also makes sense that this is what was in the mind's eye of the Apostle Peter when writing about Jesus' proclamation to "...spirits in prison" (1 Peter 3: 19).

The Proclamation

While this passage of Scripture offers considerable interpretive challenges, one thing is undeniable. Jesus, in some fashion, proclaimed something to "...the spirits *now* in prison" (1 Peter 3: 19). Yet even this plain fact raises several thought-provoking questions including:

1. What was the content of the proclamation?
2. In what form was the proclamation delivered?
3. What was unique about the antediluvians that they should be singled out as the recipients of Jesus' proclamation?

Many English Bible translations interpret *poreutheis ekēruxen* as "...he went and preached" (v. 19, KJV), but this translation arguably falls short since it leaves the impression that Jesus *preached the gospel message* to spirits in prison. The literal translation is "...having gone, He proclaimed" (Disciples Literal New Testament). The text fails to identify the gospel message as the subject of that proclamation. Generally, it is the Greek *euaggelizó*, from which the English word *evangelize* is derived, that depicts preaching of the gospel. While *ekēruxen* is occasionally used in connection with the gospel, in those cases it is commonly specified as proclaiming *the gospel* (cf. Matthew 24: 14; 26: 13; Mark 14: 9; 16: 15; 2 Corinthians 11: 4; Galatians 2: 2; Colossians 1: 23; 1 Thessalonians 2: 9).

The idea that Jesus preached the gospel to spirits in prison, presumably offering them a second chance at salvation, can be rejected for several reasons. First, elsewhere in his letter Peter touches on the preaching of the gospel twice and, in each case, it is the term *euaggelizó* that is used (1 Peter 1: 12; 4: 6). Second, the gospel message is not identified in connection with Jesus' proclamation. Third, it would run contrary to the balance of Scripture to offer the gospel message to those who have passed from this life. Finally, it is highly unlikely that a post-mortem offering of salvation would be restricted to a specific group – particularly the evil antediluvians – since God would prefer to see all of humankind saved (cf. 1 Timothy 2: 4).

The fact that it is not revealed in the text makes it difficult to know the content of Jesus' proclamation, but it may well be related to the *form* of that proclamation. Peter does not say that Jesus spoke *orally* to the spirits, but that he proclaimed. A proclamation can take many shapes and God is known for his use of actions to teach lessons. No doubt, as suggested by Dalton, the building of the ark would have served as a compelling optical statement to Noah's contemporaries. Similarly, the prophet Ezekiel was often told to perform tasks to teach the Israelites various lessons. One such act even involved the prophet displaying no signs of sorrow following the death of his wife whom he loved (Ezekiel 24: 15-27). Also, the prophet Hosea was told to marry a prostitute to reflect the unfaithfulness of the Israelites (Hosea 1: 2). Therefore, Jesus' proclamation may have come in the form of action – perhaps the very action with which it is connected in the passage.

> **The fact that it is not revealed in the text makes it difficult to know the content of Jesus' proclamation...**

Rather than teaching that Jesus traveled to a prison in the unseen world to preach either to fallen angels or to the lost souls of Noah's day, the text indicates that *going, he proclaimed*. If, as Dalton has suggested, *poreutheis* (v. 19) reflects the same journey as *poreutheis* three verses later (v. 22), which is a reasonable conclusion, then the *proclamation* to spirits in prison must be seen in that light. If it is the ascension that is in view, then the proclamation may have been a natural consequence of Jesus' *going*. In other words, he proclaimed via the ascension.

On earth, Jesus' death was marked by some startling drama including the tearing of the temple veil, an earthquake, rocks splitting in two, and a number of deceased believers being restored to life (cf. Matthew 27: 50-53). It seems likely that his death also reverberated throughout the spiritual world. He was/is, after all, the Son of God. While his resurrection and ascension were not so dramatically felt on earth, it can be inferred from Scripture that these events resounded in the unseen realm. All other-worldly beings having been made subject to him, his ascension was the moment when Jesus took his place at the Father's right hand (1 Peter 3: 22) to rule both the seen and unseen worlds.

If Jesus' ascension was the method of delivery for his proclamation, it stands to reason that it also served as the content of his message. Victory over sin and death was made manifest in the ascension as Jesus returned to the spiritual world. The ascension testified to the completion of his mission on earth and a return to his position at the Father's right hand. Consequently, Peter had no reason to reveal the details of the proclamation since the ascension and the proclamation were one.

What was special about the antediluvians that Peter should single them out as recipients of Jesus' proclamation? This is a question that has perplexed many a Bible scholar over the past two millennia. It is difficult to imagine a message that would have been intended specifically for those who lived during the building of the ark. Then again, it could be that the proclamation was not directed exclusively at certain spirits, but that it would have been met with a special profundity among those beings.

Reviewing the landscape of human history, one factor separates Noah's contemporaries from the balance of humanity. The decades preceding the flood represent the only time God pondered ending mankind's existence. His choices were to end all human life, which Scripture describes as his preliminary decision (Genesis 6: 7), or to preserve a remnant and begin again. He chose the latter and mankind continued through the line of Noah. Since Peter highlights the pre-flood generations, it makes sense that this unique circumstance could provide the key to understanding that connection.

Like the rich man in the parable (Luke 16: 19-31), it is reasonable to believe that Noah's contemporaries, who would have been awaiting the final judgment in Hádes at the time of Jesus' ascension, regretted the decisions they had made while on earth. They were *almost* responsible for the annihilation of humankind. Had that happened, men would never have known the grace that was being offered through Jesus' death and resurrection. Jesus would not have died and resurrected on mankind's behalf, and there would have been no triumphal ascension – Jesus' crowning achievement.

God chose to start over where mankind was concerned only because of Noah's faithfulness. Finally, in the first century, the fruit of God's decision was realized as Jesus, having risen from the grave, ascended to Heaven. That is a message that would have reverberated throughout the spiritual realm (cf. 1 Peter 3: 22) and most profoundly among the antediluvian community, knowing that their actions had almost cost mankind the opportunity to experience God's grace.

Chapter 8

Baptism and Ascension

1 Peter 3: 21-22

Corresponding to That

Peter's reference to "…spirits in prison" (v. 19), identified as Noah's contemporaries (v. 20), is a transitional statement. It serves as a segue to his comparison of the flood of Noah's day with baptism in the church age. According to the NASV translation, "Corresponding to that (the flood), baptism now saves you" (1 Peter 3: 21). On the one hand, it was the *type* (the flood), as the water buoyed the ark, that served as the agent in saving the physical lives of Noah and his family. In the church age, it is the *antitype* (baptism) that provides agency for spiritual life.

The type/antitype correlation appears often in Scripture and was mentioned earlier when comparing Adam (the type) and Jesus (the antitype) in Paul's letter to the Corinthians. Generally speaking, the *type* represents the physical side of the equation while the *antitype* depicts the spiritual side. The antitype is the (spiritual) mirror image of the type. Where the current text is concerned, it is the NKJV that employs this precise verbiage.

> There is also an antitype which now saves us—baptism (not the removal of the filth of the flesh, but the answer of a good conscience toward God), through the resurrection of Jesus Christ. (1 Peter 3: 21, NKJV)

Many people seem to believe that this section of Scripture is about *The Descensus*. Consequently, they mistakenly concentrate on Jesus' *proclamation to spirits in prison* (vv. 19-20) as though this is the heart of the apostle's message. However, the meaningful lesson from the text is found in the final two verses of the chapter (vv. 21-22). The comment about Noah's peers (spirits in prison) simply provides a bridge between Peter's words about Jesus' death and resurrection (v. 18) and his words about baptism (v. 21). This especially makes sense if, as scholars have determined, these words were given at a baptismal service. In establishing that connection, he recognizes the salvific effect of the flood waters, noting that "…eight persons, were brought safely through *the* water" (v. 20). In other words, God used the water to separate Noah's family from the sin and death that had engulfed their world. He then compares God's use of the flood waters to baptismal waters in the church age.

Noah and his family were saved from death as they floated on the water in the ark Noah had built. The mirror image of the salvation of Noah's family is found in one's immersion in water (the antitype). In baptism a person is submerged in the water, rather than being buoyed above the water, as a matter of salvation.

It is his words about baptism that would have provided assurance to Peter's audience, particularly for those who may have been baptized on that day. This is in keeping with both the immediate text and the larger theme of the epistle. When recognized as a transitional comment, Peter's mention of the antediluvians offers a natural fit in the flow of the narrative. It would have been both awkward and extraneous in this setting for the apostle to introduce, and then dismissively abandon, a discussion about a mysterious spiritual journey into the unseen world. A curious departure such as this could only detract from the lesson of encouragement the apostle hoped to convey.

Baptism Saves

Peter's comment that, "…baptism now saves you" (v. 21) has been the source of confusion, controversy, and high-minded debate, particularly over the course of the past several hundred years as the church experienced and emerged from the Reformation Movement of the sixteenth century. Some wonder if the apostle has errantly credited baptism with having innate powers such that anyone who is immersed in water might be saved, or spiritually regenerated.

The flood waters of Noah's day had no inherent authority to bring death to mankind. The rain was simply a creation of God. He could have ended the rain after a few days, the people having learned their lesson, but he did not. He chose to use the water as an instrument for the obliteration of evil, but the water also served as an instrument of salvation and renewal for Noah and his family. The life they had known was behind them, buried in the flood waters, and new life awaited them on the other side of the flood. This explains Peter's type/antitype comparison with baptism.

Water baptism has no inherent redemptive power or authority. Like the flood waters of old, baptism is an instrument devised by God for use in the church age. Peter recognizes the significance of the rite of baptism in that it is the time God has chosen for a person to receive forgiveness of sins (Acts 2: 38; 22: 16; Colossians 2: 11). It is at the time of submersion in water that a repentant believer leaves his/her life of sin behind and begins life anew (John 3: 5; Romans 6: 1-4; Titus 3: 5). Consequently, the apostle is correct in saying "...baptism now saves you" (1 Peter 3: 21) in that God has chosen baptism as the time for these spiritual changes (forgiveness and regeneration) to take place. These cannot be attributed to the *act* of baptism (the water has no self-contained spiritual power), but to God's work during baptism as he has established this as the *time* when he will bestow these blessings.

An Appeal

The apostle compares (flood) water to (baptismal) water, noting that the salvific character of baptism is grounded in Jesus' resurrection (v. 21). This observation concerning baptism envelops a parenthetical remark from the apostle about the *kind* of cleansing that occurs during baptism. The point of his parenthetical statement is that, while water generally serves as a cleansing agent for physical washing (dirt from the flesh), in the case of baptism it works as an agent of spiritual cleansing (forgiveness of sins). This is a lesson taught forthrightly in God's Word (Acts 2: 38; 22: 16). For this reason, Paul regards baptism as a "...washing of regeneration" (Titus 3: 5) in his letter to Titus and "...washing of water with the word" (Ephesians 5: 26) when writing to the church in Ephesus.

Submission to baptism serves as a person's appeal to God that he would, during that act, grant the promise of forgiveness that he has made for the one who submits. This is the purpose of the design of baptism (being buried and raised with Christ) and it is the idea behind the aside that Peter has inserted in the text. Having been forgiven, an individual rises from the water to begin a new life (Romans 6: 4) with a clean, sin-free conscience. It is the post-flood and post-baptism newness of life that makes them comparable.

Through the Resurrection

According to Peter, the efficacy of the rite of baptism is grounded in "...the resurrection of Jesus Christ" (v. 21). The author of the book of Hebrews wrote, "...without the shedding of blood there is no forgiveness" (Hebrews 9: 22). Consequently, the forgiveness God offers the believer is based on Jesus' death (shedding of blood). Jesus' resurrection represents the newness of life one experiences during submission to baptism. This explains why Peter has linked the changes that take place during baptism to the resurrection mentioned earlier in the text (1 Peter 3: 18).

Ascended

Having addressed Jesus' death and resurrection (v. 18), as well as baptism (v. 21), Peter states that Jesus "...is at the right hand of God, having gone into heaven, after angels and authorities and powers had been subjected to Him" (1 Peter 3: 22). This is offered by the apostle as a statement of inspiration. It speaks to ultimate victory even in the face of the suffering many believers were experiencing at the time. It also offers insight into some of the earlier verses discussed here.

Peter begins with the most inspiring comment of all, telling his readers that Jesus now sits at God's right hand and he oversees everything. This serves as support for his earlier remarks that they should not be discouraged when they are persecuted since Jesus is watching over them (vv. 14-17).

The text states, "...having gone (poreutheis) into heaven" Jesus now sits at God's right hand. Peter's identical use of the term *poreutheis* in this verse is what has led Dalton and others to conclude that the apostle was equally referring to the ascension earlier in this passage when he wrote *poreutheis ekēruxen*, which literally translates into English as "...having gone, He proclaimed" (Disciples Literal New Testament). This seems to be a reasonable conclusion and gives a much different picture of a phrase that is often translated "He went and preached" (ASV). If Jesus' *going* (v. 19) is intended to depict the ascension, it stands to reason that the ascension is meant to serve as (the form of) the proclamation.

This view is further supported by Peter's recognition that Jesus ascended "…after angels and authorities and powers had been subjected to Him" (v. 22). These words describe one of the impressive outcomes of Jesus' ministry that would have been felt across the vast expanse that is the spiritual realm. Men do not know the powerful impact Jesus' death, burial, resurrection, and ascension had on the unseen world, but it is safe to say that all in that world were aware that things had changed dramatically. His ascension marked his final earthly act and the dawn of a new day. That final act undoubtedly sent a powerful message that would have resounded through the halls of spiritual domains, serving as a declaration that Jesus had returned to his rightful place in Heaven.

> **Men do not know the powerful impact Jesus' death, burial, resurrection, and ascension had on the unseen world…**

Chapter 9

Faithful in Judgment

1 Peter 4:1-6

Changed Life

While 1 Peter 3: 22 ends the third chapter of Peter's first epistle, his train of thought remains uninterrupted. He continues with his theme of encouragement, knowing the persecution and challenges the believers faced. If this work originated with a baptismal service, it stands to reason that he wanted to prepare these new Christians for the trials they could anticipate.

The first six verses of the fourth chapter complete his thoughts on the gospel message the apostle delivered in the final five verses of the third chapter. Peter draws stark contrast between being *in the flesh* and *in the spirit*. His emphasis here is on the world of flesh since that is where people face the challenges of persecution and temptation. It is the world where these believers would remain, at least for a time, suffering for their faith.

Reiterating his point that Christ suffered (died) in the flesh (3: 18), Peter encourages his audience to "arm yourselves also with the same purpose" (4: 1). That is, be like-minded with Christ. Jesus died to wash away their sins. Those who suffer in the flesh honor Christ with that suffering since, the only reason they face persecution is that they no longer live as they had lived before accepting Jesus as savior. Their suffering serves as witness to the fact that they no longer live in sin.

Peter is clear that these Christians should expect to *remain* in the flesh (in physical form) for a time, but they should not *live* in the flesh. While they continued to live on earth, they should be faithful to God to the end. No longer would they seek after "human lusts" (v. 2). Instead, their focus should be, and must be, on seeking to do God's will, turning their backs on sins and honoring Jesus with the way they live their lives.

The Past is the Past

Living in Asia Minor during the days of the Roman Empire, these believers came from a world not unlike that of the antediluvians. Sin was rampant and fully engulfed their world. Those who accepted Christ had chosen to leave that world – the world of flesh – behind them. According to Peter, "...the time already past is sufficient *for you*" (v. 3). With these words, he was not suggesting that they had already had their fun and that it was time to stop having fun and move past that life. Rather, he was saying that having lived in that world, and having "...carried out the desire of the Gentiles, having pursued a course of indecent behavior, lusts, drunkenness, carousing, drinking parties, and wanton idolatries" (v. 3), they should fully grasp how little that life had to offer. Juxtaposed against life in Christ, they should look back at their previous life as one where lessons were learned and the road ahead, leading away from that previous life, was clear.

The fact that they had left their life of sin to follow Jesus does not mean that they no longer cared about those with whom they had been close for so long, but those relationships were certainly being tested. Speaking frankly, Peter acknowledged that those who continued to live *in the flesh*, their old friends, "...are surprised that you do not run with *them* in the same excesses of debauchery" (v. 4). In other words, their buddies from their past would ask the question: *What is wrong with you? You used to enjoy your life with us and the fun times we had.*

That kind of question eventually turned to bitterness and then anger. These old friends were no longer simply asking *why*. According to Peter "...they slander you" (v. 4). Their bitterness/anger had turned into a malignant tumor as they sought to destroy the new life the believers were experiencing in Christ. Perhaps it had become their primary focus – their mission in life – to make the lives of the believers as miserable as possible, failing to comprehend what it meant to no longer live *in the flesh*.

Judgment

These Christians surely had mixed emotions concerning their past friendships. They undoubtedly still cared about those who continued in that previous life. In fact, their awakening in Christ would have led them to care even more about their friends who had rejected Jesus. They must have shared Jesus with them, hoping they would join them in this new spiritual experience. It is clear from the text that many declined the offer.

Even though they still cared deeply for those left in the world of flesh, the maligning and persecution heaped upon the believers from their old friends would have taken its toll. Nevertheless, their frustration should not be read into Peter's words concerning judgment as though it was a matter of satisfaction for the believers. They would not have been seeking retribution for persecution. Therefore, when the apostle stated concerning those still in the world, "…they will give an account" (v. 5), these words were not spoken from the perspective of revenge, but of sorrow.

Jesus will eventually judge everyone. In fact, according to the apostle, Jesus "…is ready to judge the living and the dead" (v. 5). No human being will escape judgment in some form. Even believers will be judged (cf. 2 Corinthians 5: 10), although the judgment experienced by the faithful will be distinct from that experienced by the unfaithful. Scripture suggests that believers' lives will be assessed, perhaps even having their lives laid bare before them, as a matter of determining their measure of reward, while unbelievers will be judged as a matter of condemnation.

Preaching the Gospel

Another challenge is encountered here in a verse that, like 3: 19, has been analyzed and dissected far more than is necessary or wise. Peter's words concerning the preaching of the gospel (v. 6) indicate that some may have questioned the eternal fortune of those who never heard of Jesus' death and resurrection. These believers found solace and salvation in the gospel message, but perhaps their previous loved ones (parents, grandparents, etc.) had not. When it comes to judgment, how, then, could they be rightly judged? For that matter, how could Jesus fairly judge the countless souls who had died prior to his coming to earth or prior to the declaration of his death and resurrection? *The Cambridge Bible for Schools and Colleges* and *The Pulpit Commentary* respectively raise this question:

> The question might be asked, How were the dead to be judged by their acceptance or rejection of the Gospel when they had passed away without any opportunity of hearing it?[30]

> ...some of St. Peter's readers may, perhaps, have thought that those who had passed away before the gospel times could not be justly judged in the same way as those who then were living. The two classes, the living and the dead, were separated by a great difference: the living had heard the gospel, the dead had not; the living had opportunities and privileges which had not been granted to the dead. [31].

The apostle's words, in keeping with the theme of encouragement and inspiration, offer his audience a sense of assurance as he explained, "For the gospel has for this purpose been preached even to those who are dead, that though they are judged in the flesh as people, they may live in the spirit according to *the will of* God" (v. 6). How could the gospel have been preached prior to Christ's death and resurrection, particularly in Old Testament times? The answer lies in defining the character of that message.

In modern times, the gospel is generally understood as the sacrificial death, burial, resurrection, and ascension of a sinless Jesus to erase man's sins so that a repentant person might be suited for Heaven. The Greek term *euaggelizó* expresses the idea of bringing good tidings and is generally associated with Jesus' death and resurrection. While this is true in the church age, the Bible shows that God has consistently provided humankind with some sense of the good news modern men share, even though mankind may not have understood the link to Jesus specifically.

God's message has always been one of faith in God and obedience to his commands. That was the message delivered to Adam and Eve and is also reflected in the offerings of Cain and Abel. A comparable message was delivered to the antediluvians and to the Israelites

---

[30] *The Cambridge Bible for Schools and Colleges* https://biblehub.com/ commentaries/cambridge/1_peter/4.htm, accessed July 5, 2020.

[31] *The Pulpit Commentary*, https://biblehub.com/commentaries/pulpit/1_peter/4.htm, accessed July 5, 2020.

beginning with their father Abraham. The good tidings by which humankind might have a spiritual relationship with God permeate the pages of the Old Testament.

Every human being with the capacity to understand will have received a form of good tidings from God in his/her lifetime. While those who died before Christ appeared on earth may not have known of his death and resurrection, *per se*, each one had the opportunity to respond to the good news they received. Several commentaries are cited here since, placed together, they seem to provide a true and full explanation of the text,

> Peter, by naming Him to whom the evil-speakers shall render an account, the Judge of the quick and the dead, implies thereby that they are not to remain unpunished, whether they die before the day of judgment or not. And this, as a testimony to the justice of God, should serve to comfort the Christians under the calumnies which they had to endure, and exhort them not to be led aside by them to a denial of their Christian walk....it cannot be denied that the apostle gives expression to the thought that the gospel has been preached to all, who are dead, at the time when the last judgment arrives.[32]

> Further, the thought of Christ as the judge should both silence the blasphemers and strengthen the blasphemed to endure. That judgment will vindicate the wisdom of those who sowed to the spirit and the folly of those who sowed to the flesh. The one will reap corruption; the other, life everlasting.

> The difficult verse 6 cannot be adequately dealt with here, but we may note that introductory 'for' shows that it, too, contains a motive urging to life, 'to the will of God,' and that no such motive appears in it if it is taken to mean, as by some, that the gospel is preached after death to the dead. Surely to say that 'the gospel was preached also {or, even} to them that are dead' is not to say that it was preached to them when dead.[33]

> It is His judging that is linked with verse 6, and helps to rid it of the difficulties with which superstition loads and darkens it. "For to this end the glad tidings went to dead persons also, that they might be judged according to men in flesh, and live according to God in spirit." From the hour that man fell by sin under death and judgment, God had in His grace a gospel to shelter and give life according to God; which is therefore in the last book of scripture called "an everlasting gospel." To this clung faith from the first; and it was added to

---

[32] Meyer, Frederick B., https://biblehub.com/commentaries/meyer/1_peter/4.htm, accessed July 5, 2020.

[33] MacLaren, Alexander, https://biblehub.com/commentaries/maclaren/1_peter/4.htm, accessed July 5, 2020.

and cleared gradually throughout the O.T. till the death, resurrection, and glory of Christ gave it fulness.[34]

They are dead, but to every generation of them was the Gospel preached, that God might gather Him a great multitude to stand on His right hand in the day of account.[35]

Some may wonder if this text, where Peter writes about the dead having received good tidings (4: 6), offers a modicum of support for Augustine's view that Jesus, in the spirit, spoke through Noah as he built the ark. Could it be that the verses discussed earlier are meant to characterize Jesus speaking through Noah in his *proclamation to the spirits in prison* (3: 19-20)? In fact, it is fair to say that Jesus spoke through Noah at the time, but it is unlikely that this is the proclamation of which the apostle speaks in this setting. The sequencing of events in the third chapter of 1 Peter portrays Jesus' proclamation taking place after his resurrection and not in the days of Noah.

---

[34] Kelly, William, *William Kelly Major Works Commentary*, https://biblehub.com/commentaries/kelly/1_peter/4.htm, accessed July 5, 2020.
[35] *Expositor's Bible Commentary*, https://biblehub.com/commentaries/expositors/1_peter/4.htm, accessed July 5, 2020.

Section 3

Surveying The Biblical Landscape

Chapter 10
Perusing Scripture

Addressing God's Word

The belief that Jesus descended into Hell became official dogma in the Roman Catholic Church when it was incorporated into the Apostles' Creed in the seventh century – a decision that has heavily affected doctrinal perspective (Purgatory, etc.) in modern Christendom. The reason this has proven to be so influential is that, according to surveys, few people read the Bible regularly and even fewer engage in the study of challenging topics where Scripture is concerned. Most who read the Bible on a regular basis do so as a matter of devotional guidance or to seek spiritual inspiration. Grappling with some of the more obscure issues, such as what Jesus may have done spiritually between his death and resurrection, is generally left to professional Bible scholars who, in turn, offer their views to those who will listen. Consequently, few people are aware of what the Bible has to say about such matters.

The fact that people derive much of their doctrinal beliefs from contemporary teachers rather than Scripture has influenced the biblical perspectives of many believers. Having decided what they believe about a certain topic based purely upon what they have learned from others, when they turn to Scripture and encounter passages where a specific subject is addressed, every verse is read through the lens of preconception. This is often the case when it comes to the topic of Jesus' spiritual activity as his body lay in the tomb.

In addition to the words of the Apostle Peter about Jesus *proclaiming to the spirits in prison* (1 Peter 3: 19), discussed in detail in the previous section, a multitude of Bible verses have been offered as support for assorted beliefs about the time between Jesus' death and resurrection. Beyond 1 Peter, dozens of biblical passages have been utilized to argue that after his physical death Jesus did, indeed, journey to the spiritual domain known as Hell. Some of these verses are repetitive, so it is unnecessary to address each one in detail, but it will help to consider some of the primary texts that are employed to make that case.

The Old Testament

Those who were not aware prior to reading this book must now realize that Hell is not mentioned by the Old Testament writers. Nonetheless, there are those who seek to use certain Old Testament writings to make the case that Jesus traveled to Hell. These passages are often presented as prophecies concerned with the activities of the coming Messiah,

Five Old Testament passages will be addressed in the following pages since they are the primary passages used to make the argument. These include Psalm 16: 10-11; 71: 20; 88: 10-12; Ezekiel 26: 20; and Hosea 13: 14. Other Old Testament verses that come into play generally repeat in some fashion what is said in these verses, so the explanations given here can be equally applied in those cases.

The New Testament

The New Testament offers a much greater opportunity to derive lessons about Hell since this spiritual domain is mentioned there. However, this does not change the fact that doctrine about Jesus descending to Hell can only be derived through inference since no verse or passage states overtly that Jesus made such a journey. The word Hell (Gehenna) appears fifteen times in the New Testament, but not one of those fifteen verses has been offered by scholars to influence belief regarding Jesus' descent.

Several New Testament verses have been loosely interpreted to make the case concerning Jesus descending into Hell. Five passages have been selected here that are representative of the arguments that have been offered. These include Matthew 12: 38-40; Acts 2: 24-35; Romans 10: 6-7; Ephesians 4: 7-14; and Revelation 1: 18.

This section ends with a chapter entitled "Peering Behind the Stone" where an attempt is made to offer a purely biblical look into the time following Jesus' death. What occurred during those days is not completely unknown since Scripture offers some subtle guidance. However, it is unwise to wander beyond the words of Scripture to develop doctrine, mixing biblical and non-biblical works as a matter of speculation. Therefore, consideration of Jesus' time in the tomb will be limited to what God has offered through his inspired writers.

Chapter 11

Psalm 16:10-11

Your Holy One

King David, who penned much of the Psalms, often wrote concerning the coming Messiah who would be his direct descendent. One powerful example is found in Psalm 16 where he wrote the following:

> [10] For You will not abandon my soul to Sheol;
> You will not allow Your Holy One to undergo decay.
> [11] You will make known to me the way of life;
> In Your presence is fullness of joy;
> In Your right hand there are pleasures forever. (Psalm 16: 10-11)

Some have read into this passage lessons that are absent from the text. For instance, certain scholars have insisted that David was writing about himself, self-identifying as "Your Holy One" (v. 10). The purported lesson is that he anticipated living to a ripe old age. It is unlikely, though, that David, whom God identified as "...a man after My heart" (Acts 13: 22), would act so presumptuously as to call himself holy, particularly given his history of adultery and murder. Others have attempted to interpret *chsid'k* in plural form, as though David was referring to *your holy ones*, but the Hebrew is undeniably singular. According to Ellicott:

> The received Heb. text has the word in the plural, but with the marginal note that the sign of the plural is superfluous. The weight of MS. authority of all

the ancient versions, and of the quotations Acts 2:27; Acts 13:35, is for the singular.[36]

Scripture itself refutes each of these interpretations. The term *Holy One* appears several times in the New Testament, (Mark 1: 24; Luke 4: 34; John 6: 69; Acts 3: 14; 1 Peter 1: 15; 1 John 2: 20; Revelation 16: 5) and on each of these occasions it is an incontrovertible reference to the Messiah. The expression *holy ones* appears once where it is clearly plural in form as Jude reflects on a prophecy from Enoch who stated that "…the Lord came with many thousands of His holy ones" (Jude 1: 14).

The fact that the expression *Holy One*, in the New Testament, always serves as a reference to Christ, should be sufficient to determine that, in the Psalm text, it carries the same meaning. Yet, God has provided even more evidence concerning the identity of the Holy One. Luke records both Peter (Acts 2: 27) and Paul (Acts 13: 35) citing the Psalm passage and applying the term to Jesus.

Not Abandoned to She'ol

There has been some reliance on this passage to support the argument that Jesus journeyed to Hell during his time in the grave, but this explanation of the passage is based on a misunderstanding of the words of the text. This is one of those instances in the Old Testament when the KJV translators chose to interpret the word *She'ol* as *Hell*. Consequently, many were left with the impression that, since "Your Holy One" is intended to depict Christ, it must be true that Jesus visited Hell while in the spiritual world following his death.

The meaning of *She'ol* was discussed earlier, and it is not Hell. It is, at various times, a depiction of either the grave, the realm of the dead, or a spiritual waiting place for those who have passed from this life. While any, or all, of these could apply here, in this setting the most reasonable view is that *She'ol* points to the physical grave. This seems to be the message David hoped to convey in this prophecy concerning the Messiah. As the whole of the text is considered, it is a picture of someone dying and rising to life again before the body has a chance to decay (vv. 10-11). Some scholars interpret David's words as a reference

---

[36] Ellicott, Charles J., *Ellicott's Commentary for English Readers*, https://www.studylight.org/Commentaries/ebc/psalms-16 accessed August 24, 2020.

to both the realm of the dead (a spiritual waiting place) and the grave while others believe it is strictly the physical grave that is in view.

> As to leaving the soul In Hell, it can only mean permitting the life of the Messiah to continue under the power of death; for שאול sheol signifies a pit, a ditch, the grave, or state of the dead.[37]

> For thou wilt not leave my soul in Hell - not the place of torment; nor, on the other hand, merely the grave, which is not referred to until the next clause; but the unseen world of disembodied souls: the Hebrew Sheol, the Greek Hades.[38]

> **In Hell** - - לשאול *lishe'ôl* "to Sheol." See Psalm 6:5, note; Isaiah 5:14, note. This word does not necessarily mean Hell in the sense in which that term is now commonly employed, as denoting the abode of the wicked in the future world, or the place of punishment; but it means the region or abode of the dead, to which the grave was regarded as the door or entrance - the underworld. The idea is, that the soul would not be suffered to remain in that underworld - that dull, gloomy abode (compare the notes at Job 10:21-22), but would rise again to light and life. This language, however, gives no sanction to the words used in the creed, "he descended into Hell," nor to the opinion that Christ went down personally to "preach to the spirits in prison " - the souls that are lost (compare the notes at 1 Peter 3:19)[39]

Those who seek to portray Psalm 16 as an example of Jesus descending to Hell have drawn from the text a lesson that cannot be found in David's words. The passage states in simple terms that Jesus died and rose again. It is the heart of the gospel message that is in view here. There is no allusion to Jesus' spiritual activity between his death and resurrection.

---

[37] Clarke, Adam, *Clarke's Commentary Volume III: Book of Job-Song of Solomon*, Abingdon-Cokesbury Press, New York-Nashville, p. 265.
[38] Jamieson, Robert, Fausset, A. R. and Brown, David, *A Commentary on the Old and New Testaments Volume 2: Job-Malachi*, Hendrickson Publishers, Peabody, MA, 2008, p. 134.
[39] Barnes, Albert, *Albert Barnes' Notes on the Whole Bible*, https://www.studylight.org/commentaries/bnb/psalms-16.html, accessed August 24, 2020.

Chapter 12
Psalm 71: 20

Revival

The Psalms are filled with language that is poetic, prophetic, and inspirational, as is evident in the text that was addressed in the previous chapter (Psalm 16: 10-11), which is both prophetic and inspirational. In that passage, it is the death and resurrection of Christ that is in view. The same is true of the following passage.

> You who have shown me many troubles and distresses
> Will revive me again,
> And will bring me up again from the depths of the earth. (Psalm 71: 20)

Like the text in the previous chapter, this passage focuses on the heart of the gospel message – Jesus' death and resurrection. It points to Jesus being revived from death, or the grave. Yet, some have turned to these words to defend their belief in *The Descensus*. How could this verse be used in such a way? The teaching leans heavily on the expression "…depths of the earth."

It may be worded a bit differently in assorted English translations, but the phrase appears several times in Scripture. In the Old Testament, this expression is translated from various Hebrew phrases. For instance, in the current text it is translated from *u·m·themuth e·artz*, meaning *from the abysses of the earth*. Earlier in the Psalms the phrase comes from *b·thchthiuth e·artz*, which is best translated *in the nether-parts of the earth* (Psalm 63: 9). This same Hebrew phrase is also used a bit later (Psalm 139: 15). It is occasionally rendered "…the lower parts of the earth" (Isaiah 44: 23; Ezekiel 26: 20; 32: 24). Elsewhere in the Psalms, this same English wording is derived from *mchqri – artz* which literally translates into *far depths of the earth* (Psalm 95: 4). In the NASV, the expression "…lower parts of the earth" (Ephesians 4: 9) appears once in the New Testament and comes from the Greek *katōtera merē tēs gēs*.

The terminology "…depths of the earth" in Psalm 71 fails to support the teaching that Jesus journeyed to Hell since these words do not reference Hell. Where these words appear elsewhere in Scripture, there is no hint that they serve as a reference to Hell. In fact, other biblical uses of this phraseology fully undermine that teaching. For instance, in Psalm 139: 15, this phrasing is used specifically to identify the womb of birth where David's life was formed. On the occasions where the wording is linked to death, or resurrection, the most reasonable understanding is that it is the grave that is in view – not Hell.

Chapter 13
Psalm 88: 10-12

Wonders for the Dead

Not every Psalm was written by King David. For example, some of the Psalms have been recognized as the work of sons of Korah (Psalm 42; 44; 45; 46; 47; 48; 49; 84; 85; 87; 88). Some of this group, who were descendants of a man who was a contemporary of Moses (cf. Exodus 6: 21-24), developed into professional musicians. The Psalms listed here were evidently authored by some of these musicians in the form of lyrics. A Psalm penned by one of the sons of Korah is also considered by many to offer an allusion to Jesus' journey to Hell. In that Psalm it is written:

> [10] Will You perform wonders for the dead?
> Or will the departed spirits rise *and* praise You? *Selah*
> [11] Will Your graciousness be declared in the grave,
> Your faithfulness in Abaddon?
> [12] Will Your wonders be made known in the darkness?
> And Your righteousness in the land of forgetfulness? (Psalm 88: 10-12)

Taken out of context, it is easy to see why someone might mistake this for a prophecy about Jesus visiting the dead. Yet, that conclusion is only possible when the circumstance behind the writing of these verses is ignored.

At Death's Door

The name of the author of Psalm 88 is unknown, but he was in a difficult situation. He was evidently quite ill and believed the end of his life was near. In his affliction, he appealed to God about his dilemma and what he believed he faced in death. This is explained in the first few verses of the Psalm where he wrote:

> ¹ LORD, the God of my salvation,
> I have cried out by day and in the night before You.
> ² Let my prayer come before You;
> Incline Your ear to my cry!
> ³ For my soul has had enough troubles,
> And my life has approached Sheol.
> ⁴ I am counted among those who go down to the pit;
> I have become like a man without strength (Psalm 88: 1-4)

The setting in this Psalm gives a different perspective when considering those verses that have so often been cited in support of Jesus journeying to Hell. In fact, when given honest consideration, it becomes clear that the meaning of the text contradicts the notion that Jesus descended to Hell.

The Psalm tells the story of a man who is pleading for his life. Questions like, "Will You perform wonders for the dead?" (v. 10) are rhetorical in nature. The author believed he would soon die and spent time here appealing to God as he contemplated the realities of the grave. The question asked is not a question. It is a comment, recognizing that wonders *are not* performed for those in the grave. Barnes explains it with the following observations:

> The wonders - or the things suited to excite admiration - which the living behold. Shall the dead see those things which here tend to excite reverence for thee, and which lead people to worship thee? The idea is that the dead will be cut off from all the privileges which attend the living on earth; or, that those in the grave cannot contemplate the character and the greatness of God.[40]

The example of this Psalm reveals the importance of considering context when determining the meaning of a verse or passage of Scripture. Failure to honestly consider the circumstance behind the

---

[40] Barnes, Albert, *Albert Barnes' Notes on the Whole Bible*, https://www.studylight.org/commentaries/bnb/psalms-88.html, accessed August 29, 2020.

writing can lead to specious conclusions such as the claim that this passage portrays Jesus visiting Hell.

Chapter 14
Ezekiel 26: 20

Down to the Pit...Lower Parts of the Earth

Over the course of the past few chapters, it has been noted that the Old Testament expression *the pit*, along with the phrase *lower parts of the earth*, are often presented as prophetic evidence of Jesus' visit to the souls in Hell. One verse in Ezekiel, it is said, strengthens the argument in favor of Jesus journeying to Hell since the terms appear together and the verse purportedly speaks of Jesus *remaining* in the lower parts of the earth.

> ...then I will bring you down with those who go down to the pit, to the people of old, and I will make you remain in the lower parts of the earth, like the ancient ruins, with those who go down to the pit, so that you will not be inhabited; but I will put glory in the land of the living. (Ezekiel 26: 20)

Once again, context refutes the notion that this is a prophecy concerning the Messiah traveling to Hell after his death. In the twenty-sixth chapter of Ezekiel, God is condemning the city of Tyre. With Jerusalem defenseless, the people of Tyre sought to be opportunists. This reality is explained in the first few verses of the chapter where the background behind the prophecy in this verse is revealed.

> [1]Now in the eleventh year, on the first of the month, the word of the LORD came to me, saying, [2] "Son of man, because Tyre has said in regard to Jerusalem, 'Aha! The gateway of the peoples is broken; it has opened to me. I shall be filled, *now that* she is laid waste,' [3] therefore this is what the

Lord GOD says: 'Behold, I am against you, Tyre, and I will bring up many nations against you, as the sea brings up its waves. (Ezekiel 26: 1-3)

These verses reveal the theme of the chapter. God was looking at punishing the people of Tyre for their wanton disregard for God and his people and for the special role of Jerusalem, which they knew was considered a holy city, in God's plans.

Comparison to Antediluvians

Scholars generally agree that the prophet's warning that the people of Tyre would "go down to the pit, to the people of old" references the antediluvians who died in the flood. To a degree, God, through the prophet Ezekiel, compared their scandalous plans and deeds with what most would consider the vilest of all generations. The heart of the message is that the people of Tyre could anticipate a similar fate as it is described in the text:

> For this is what the Lord GOD says: "When I make you a desolate city, like the cities which are not inhabited, when I bring up the deep over you and the great waters cover you, (Ezekiel 26: 19)

Ezekiel's comparison of the fate of Tyre to the time of the flood sounds ominous, but it is also very fitting. Coffman explains the similarity with a strikingly pointed observation.

> This suggests an obvious analogy. That godless world that lived prior to the Great Deluge was covered with the "great waters," even as the rains of Tyre were scraped into the sea and the "great waters" covered them, thus providing for Tyre, "Its everlasting dwelling-place, among the rains of that primeval world which was destroyed by the flood, and beside that godless race of the Ante-Diluvians."[41]

As far as *remaining* in *the lower parts of the earth* is concerned (v. 20), it is reasonable to believe that this, as with other such references, points to the fact the those who are in view would, indeed, die and this expression, along with the term *the pit*, alludes to the grave, She'ol, or the realm of the dead. Any one of these would fit comfortably with the imagery found in Ezekiel's words.

---

[41] Coffman, James B., *Coffman's Commentaries on the Bible*, https://studylight.org/commentaries/bcc/Ezekiel-26.html., accessed August 31, 2020.

Honest regard for context is vital when it comes to understanding text, and this is especially true where Scripture is concerned since God's Word is intended to serve as a guide for mankind. When context is given due consideration, this verse falls well short of providing support for the belief that Jesus descended to Hell.

Chapter 15
Hosea 13:14

Redemption from Death

It has been said that the following text from Hosea depicts Jesus rescuing souls from Hell, presumably as his spirit traversed there after his death on the cross.

> Shall I ransom them from the power of Sheol?
> Shall I redeem them from death?
> O Death, where are your thorns?
> O Sheol, where is your sting?
> Compassion will be hidden from My sight. (Hosea 13: 14)

Even a questionable KJV rendering cannot be blamed for the misconception arising from this text. The responsibility falls squarely on the shoulders of those who choose to teach what the text does not. In this case, the KJV rightly translates She'ol as grave.

> I will ransom them from the power of the grave; I will redeem them from death: O death, I will be thy plagues; O grave, I will be thy destruction: repentance shall be hid from mine eyes. (Hosea 13: 14, KJV)

In this instance, the prophet Hosea writes of Ephraim – both the individual (son of Joseph) and the Hebrew tribe that bore his name. Unlike his father, Ephraim suffered from the affliction of pride and haughtiness, a trait that was evidently reflected in his descendants.

While the prophet seems to focus on Ephraim, he is but an example. This chapter spells punishment not only for the tribe of Ephraim, but for

Israel generally (v. 9). They had followed Ephraim's lead, constantly creating and constructing idols whom they would worship (v. 2). Over the ages the nation continually rejected God and that unfaithfulness could not go unpunished.

While Hosea seems to write of Israel's *eternal* destruction, the promise of salvation through a Hebrew Messiah lay at the heart of God's plan. How would Israel's punishment effect that plan? Would the world be eternally lost due to Israel's sins? These are the questions that are asked and answered here. Death could not prevail. This is the implication of the ransom for death found in the prophet's words. Paul cites verse 14 in his first letter to the Corinthians, reflecting upon Jesus' payment (ransom) for the sins of men, writing:

> WHERE, O DEATH, IS YOUR VICTORY? WHERE, O DEATH, IS YOUR STING?
> (1 Corinthians 15: 55)

Some believe the passage from the prophet Hosea speaks only of punishment, but the subtle message is one of redemption. Despite the Israelites' unfaithfulness, God would remain faithful to the promise he had made to Abraham. He would pay the ransom necessary to redeem men from their sins.

Nothing in the words or context of this verse could legitimately lead to the conclusion that Jesus journeyed to Hell between his death and resurrection. Once again, a passage that reflects the gospel message has been misread as a lesson about Jesus descending to Hell.

Chapter 16
Matthew 12: 38-40

The Sign of Jonah

While on earth in human form, Jesus performed many miraculous works. He healed the sick (Matthew 8: 1-3), cast out demons (Matthew 8: 28-34), calmed storms (Matthew 8: 23-27), and raised the dead (John 11: 38-44), along with other extraordinary deeds. So remarkable were these acts that people often followed him in hopes of seeing a miracle.

Over the two centuries prior to Jesus' birth, the Pharisees had become a sinister group of pseudo religious leaders. When Jesus arrived on the scene in Israel, they felt threatened and did their best to bring division between Jesus and the Jewish people. On one occasion, in an apparent effort to mock Jesus before the people, they asked him to perform a miracle.

> [38] Then some of the scribes and Pharisees said to Him, "Teacher, we want to see a sign from You." [39] But He answered and said to them, "An evil and adulterous generation craves a sign; and *so* no sign will be given to it except the sign of Jonah the prophet; [40] for just as JONAH WAS IN THE STOMACH OF THE SEA MONSTER FOR THREE DAYS AND THREE NIGHTS, so will the Son of Man be in the heart of the earth for three days and three nights. (Matthew 12: 38-40)

When Jesus performed miracles during his ministry, they always served to further his work among the people. Healings, etc., were not intended to provide a side show for onlookers. For the most part, it was not Jesus' unnatural works that attracted his followers; it was his authenticity and powerful teaching. This was a truth the Pharisees could not seem to overcome, try as they might. Asking Jesus to perform a miracle purely as a matter of entertainment was an attempt to erode his high esteem among the people.

In response, Jesus referred to his challengers as "An evil and adulterous generation…" (v. 39). He then responded to the Pharisees' request by promising them a sign they could not have anticipated. He told them the only sign they would receive would be "…the sign of Jonah the prophet" (v. 40). He explained that just as Jonah had been in the belly of a sea monster for three days and three nights, "…so will the Son of Man be in the heart of the earth for three days and three nights" (v. 40). Modern-day Christians understand Jesus' words. He was prophesying about his own death, burial, and resurrection through a type/antitype correlative.

Heart of the Earth

With the words, "…in the heart of the earth," Christ has in view his days in the tomb after his crucifixion. This truth is accepted by scholars of varying doctrinal persuasions and has been since the days of the apostles.

Insistence that assorted passages of Scripture teach that Hell is located beneath the earth's surface, purportedly around the earth's core, has led some to believe that "…in the heart of the earth" depicts Jesus descending to Hell. The claim is inferential, but non-substantive. The text says nothing about Jesus making such a journey and the spiritual underworld is not mentioned.

Jonah's days in the belly of a sea monster served as a foreshadowing of Jesus' days in the tomb. This is the only reasonable conclusion that can be drawn from the text. As has been discussed at length, it is common to find elements of the Old Testament that are reflected in New Testament events. On this occasion, there is nothing about Jonah's time in the belly of the sea monster that would direct one's attention to the fires of Hell.

> **Jonah's days in the belly of a sea monster served as a foreshadowing of Jesus' days in the tomb.**

The notion that Jesus might be prophesying about a spiritual journey to Hell would serve no purpose in this instance since the Pharisees would have no means of sorting that out. In fact, they likely failed to understand the simple meaning of the tomb, much less an ambiguous allusion to an unseen journey to a spiritual domain.

Nothing about the context of these verses suggests that Jesus might be referencing a place of eternal punishment. Given their obtuse Pharisaic nature it is unlikely that the Pharisees ever fully understood Jesus' meaning, though it stands to reason that his early followers would have eventually connected his words to the resurrection.

Chapter 17

Acts 2: 24-35

The Agony of Death

Peter's sermon on the Day of Pentecost represents not only a momentous episode in Scripture, but a turning point in the history of mankind. This was the first post-ascension proclamation of the gospel message to humankind, marking the birth of the church age in the covenant of grace. The apostle's words captivated the crowd as he offered a stunning verbal pictorial of Jesus death, burial, and resurrection to the thousands who were gathered in Jerusalem on that day. The fact that each one in the crowd was able to hear Peter's words in his own language made the message even more compelling.

The purpose of Peter's sermon was twofold. He sought first to bring awareness to his listeners that they had crucified the very savior for whom they had been waiting for so long. He emphasized the agony Jesus experienced and their own guilty participation in his crucifixion. He then sought to offer a positive message of eternal salvation based on Jesus' sacrifice of a sinless life. While the telling of Jesus' death was undoubtedly heart-breaking, the teaching was well-received as the people clamored for instruction, asking the apostles, "Brothers, what are we to do?" (Acts 2: 37). It is safe to say, given the fact that roughly three thousand people were added to the church that day, that Peter's words struck the right chord.

Certain words spoken by Peter in his sermon on the Day of Pentecost have been cited by those who insist that Jesus' descended to Hell between his death and resurrection. Toward the end of his sermon, Peter cites Psalm 16: 10, a passage that was discussed in depth earlier in this work.[42] However, the apostle offers additional information on the Day of Pentecost that can help provide clearer perspective on the meaning of the Psalm text. As he was bringing his sermon to a close, Peter cited the Old Testament passage, telling the crowd of the triumphant resurrection of the Messiah they had wrongly crucified.

> [24] But God raised Him *from the dead*, putting an end to the agony of death, since it was impossible for Him to be held in its power. [25] For David says of Him,
>
> 'I SAW THE LORD CONTINUALLY BEFORE ME,
> BECAUSE HE IS AT MY RIGHT HAND, SO THAT I WILL NOT BE SHAKEN.
> [26] THEREFORE MY HEART WAS GLAD AND MY TONGUE WAS OVERJOYED;
> MOREOVER MY FLESH ALSO WILL LIVE IN HOPE;
> [27] FOR YOU WILL NOT ABANDON MY SOUL TO HADES,
> NOR WILL YOU ALLOW YOUR HOLY ONE TO UNDERGO DECAY.
> (Acts 2: 24-27)

For many, the words, "YOU WILL NOT ABANDON MY SOUL TO HADES" stir up thoughts of *The Descensus*. Some attempt to use it to defend that doctrine but, as was mentioned earlier in a discussion of the Psalm passage that Peter has cited (Chapter 11), this text says nothing about Jesus descending to Hell. Remember that Hádes is not Hell.

The Juxtaposition

In the context of Peter's sermon on the Day of Pentecost, both in the original Psalm and Peter's citing of that Psalm, the best case can be made that Hádes speaks, not of a spiritual waiting chamber, but to the grave, or to death itself – a use of this term (or Heb. *She'ol*) that is seen throughout Scripture. This is true for a couple of reasons. First of all, the mention of physical decay directs one's attention to the grave, or death, rather than a domain where a person's spirit might remain in waiting. Second, as Peter continues his thoughts on the Day of Pentecost, he juxtaposes Jesus' time in Hádes against David's place in his grave.

---

[42] See Chapter 10, p. 80.

²⁹ "Brothers, I may confidently say to you regarding the patriarch David that he both died and was buried, and his tomb is with us to this day. ³⁰ So because he was a prophet and knew that God had sworn to him with an oath to seat *one* of his descendants on his throne, ³¹ he looked ahead and spoke of the resurrection of the Christ, that He was neither abandoned to Hades, nor did His flesh suffer decay. ³² *It is* this Jesus *whom* God raised up, *a fact* to which we are all witnesses. ³³ Therefore, since He has been exalted at the right hand of God, and has received the promise of the Holy Spirit from the Father, He has poured out this which you both see and hear. ³⁴ For it was not David who ascended into heaven, but he himself says:

'THE LORD SAID TO MY LORD,
"SIT AT MY RIGHT HAND,
³⁵ UNTIL I MAKE YOUR ENEMIES A FOOTSTOOL FOR YOUR FEET."'
(Acts 2: 29-35)

Unlike David, whose body remained in his tomb even as Peter spoke on the Day of Pentecost, Jesus' body had been raised from the dead. David's body saw decay over the centuries. In contrast, Jesus' body did not experience any decay.

The apostle's point is not that Jesus' journeyed to a spiritual domain called Hádes, but that he rose from the grave. Consequently, this text fails to provide support for the doctrine of *The Descensus* on two counts. It does not depict Jesus descending to Hell, and no honest reading of the text would lead to that conclusion. Neither does it suggest that Jesus journeyed to the spiritual domain known as Hádes, as depicted in the storyline of Lazarus and the rich man. It is only Jesus' physical death that is in view in the apostle's or the Psalmist's words.

Chapter 18
Romans 10: 6-7

The Abyss

Paul may have caused a bit of confusion with his use of the term *the abyss* when writing to the Romans. In this instance, as he loosely cited an oration of Moses from Deuteronomy, he seems to have used the term figuratively to depict death, or the grave.

> [6] But the righteousness based on faith speaks as follows: "DO NOT SAY IN YOUR HEART, 'WHO WILL GO UP INTO HEAVEN?' (that is, to bring Christ down), [7] or 'Who will descend into the abyss?' (that is, to bring Christ up from the dead). (Romans 10: 6-7)

Paul was writing hypothetically and hyperbolically about the absurdity of human beings attempting to snatch Jesus from the unseen world and bring him into this physical world that he might accomplish the things they expect of him. This should not be misunderstood as a suggestion that Jesus journeyed to Tartarus, or what Paul calls the abyss. People have no access to the unseen world, save through death. Even then, no human being can assert authority in that world, much less, bring Jesus back into the physical world. Albert Barnes and James Burton Coffman wrote the following respectively concerning this text:

> Revelation 11:7; Revelation 17:8; Revelation 20:1, Revelation 20:3. In these places the word means the deep, awful regions of the nether world. The word stands opposed to heaven; as deep as that is high; as dark as that is light; while the one is as vast as the other. In the place before us it is opposed to heaven; and to descend there to bring up one, is supposed to be as impossible as to

ascend to heaven to bring one down. Paul does not affirm that Christ descended to those regions; but he says that there is no such difficulty in religion as if one were required to descend into those profound regions to call back a departed spirit.[43]

The taunting question regarding his coming up from the grave grew out of the fact that, when Jesus rose from the dead, he did not appear to his enemies at all, but only to his disciples. The reference to bringing Christ down from heaven was an echo of the disbelief that refused to see in our Lord the miracle of the incarnation. Putting the cavil all together, we may understand the enemies as saying, "All right, if Jesus is the Messiah, bring him down from heaven, or up from the grave, and let him lead our nation in throwing off the yoke of Roman bondage." The Jewish hierarchy seemed perpetually unaware that any such thing as an earthly kingdom was not in God's plan at all.[44]

The Jewish Perspective

Prior to Jesus' birth, many, and perhaps most Israelites anticipated a messiah who would free them from the bondage of the Roman Empire and establish an earthly kingdom for the Jews that would be superior to all other earthly kingdoms. Perhaps they even believed they would rule the world, God having subjected all other kingdoms to them due to their covenantal relationship with him.

Paul explained that, even though they had hoped for an earthly kingdom, that was not what God had in mind. He emphasized the absurdity of that position by asking who among them planned to enter the spiritual world and return Jesus to earth to do their bidding. When seen from this perspective, this text not only fails to place Jesus in Hell, but identifies Paul's own sense of humor, which is often missed when reading his letters to the churches.

---

[43] Barnes, Albert, *Albert Barnes' Notes on the Whole Bible*, https://www.studylight.org/commentaries/eng/bnb/romans-10.html. accessed February 6, 2021.
[44] Coffman, James B., *James Burton Coffman Commentaries, Romans, Volume 6*, A.C.U. Press, Houtson TX, 1973, p. 348

Chapter 19
Ephesians 4: 7-14

Grace

In his letter to the church in Ephesus, in a passage that was examined briefly in the third chapter during a discussion of spiritual domains, the Apostle Paul offers some insight into gifts men have received from Christ. While certain individual spiritual gifts are mentioned in the text, the primary gift is that of grace. Within the framework of his remarks, he measures Jesus' victory against an Old Testament passage that speaks to the rewards of great triumph with his ascension portrayed as the consummation of his victory.

[7]But to each one of us grace was given according to the measure of Christ's gift. [8]Therefore it says,

"WHEN HE ASCENDED ON HIGH,
HE LED CAPTIVE *THE* CAPTIVES,
AND HE GAVE GIFTS TO PEOPLE."

[9](Now this *expression*, "He ascended," what does it mean except that He also had descended into the lower parts of the earth? [10]He who descended is Himself also He who ascended far above all the heavens, so that He might fill all things.) [11]And He gave some *as* apostles, some *as* prophets, some *as* evangelists, some *as* pastors and teachers, [12]for the equipping of the saints for the work of ministry, for the building up of the body of Christ; [13]until we all attain to the unity of the faith, and of the knowledge of the Son of God, to a mature man, to the measure of the stature which belongs to the fullness of Christ. [14]As a result, we are no longer to be children, tossed here and there by waves and carried about by every wind of

doctrine, by the trickery of people, by craftiness in deceitful scheming. (Ephesians 4: 7-14)

Jesus' ascension is significant for several reasons, not the least of which is the fact that after his ascension, the Holy Spirit took his position as comforter and teacher here on earth for the church age. Without the Holy Spirit's presence, the gifts of apostleship, prophet, etc., would not have been realized. These, along with grace, represent gifts given to men.

There has been a long-standing assertion that the statement "…He also descended into the lower parts of the earth?" (v. 9) serves as the apostle's depiction of Jesus' journey into Hell following his crucifixion, but prior to his resurrection from the tomb. The claim is built on inference since the term *Hell* does not appear in the text. Certain key terms in this passage must be fully considered to determine whether or not this is the message Paul intended.

The idea Paul has presented is not complicated. He has turned a phrase to explain the inescapable logic of Christ's ascent. In verse nine, the apostle recognizes in simple terms that 1) Jesus ascended to Heaven from earth after his resurrection and 2) since, as God's son, Heaven was Jesus' point of origin, he must have first descended to earth from Heaven. This is what one derives from a natural reading of the text. The apostle John used comparable, albeit much clearer wording in his gospel to make this same point, stating that "No one has ascended into heaven, except He who descended from heaven: the Son of Man" (John 3: 13). There is no reason to read more into the text than this. Still, it may help to give slightly deeper consideration to Paul's words.

He Ascended

Bible scholars generally agree that the expression, "He ascended" (v. 9) is a straightforward reference to Jesus' return to God the Father in his post-resurrected state (cf. John 20: 17; Acts 1: 9-11). That meaning is clarified twice within the framework of the passage itself.

In verse eight, the apostle refers to Psalm 68: 18 in drawing attention to the ascension of Christ. While there are reasonable arguments that, in its Old Testament context, the Psalm text points to something other than Christ's ascension – perhaps the victorious movement of the Ark of the Covenant from Kirjath-jearim to Mount Zion – Paul uses the passage here to depict the Messiah. He evidently believed the Psalmist's words were analogous to the coming Messiah and his ultimate ascension (v. 9). Therefore, the movement of the Ark might be considered a *type* of Christ's ascension. Others view the Psalm text as strictly forward-looking, having the ascension of Christ fully in view. Either way, given the Holy Spirit's inspiration of both verses, the Psalm passage clearly reflects upon Jesus' ascension.

What did Paul mean by the phrase "He led captive *the* captives" (v. 8)? This is understood to be a term of triumph. Comparable wording appears in other passages (cf. Isaiah 20: 4; 2 Corinthians 2: 14). The idea is that the conqueror frees those who had been captured by his enemy and/or he takes the leaders of his conquered enemies into captivity. In the case of Jesus' resurrection and ascension, both ideas would apply. Sin and death had been conquered and led into bondage (cf. Romans 6: 8-11) while those who had been enslaved by sin were freed from their captivity (cf. Romans 6: 5-7, 17-18).

Paul further clarifies the term "He ascended" in verse ten, noting that Jesus "…ascended far above all the Heavens, so that he might fill all things." Therefore, the ascension mentioned in these verses can only be Christ's ascension that is described elsewhere in God's Word (John 3: 13: 20: 4; Acts 1: 9-11).

He Descended

The fact that Jesus descended to earth from Heaven is indisputable, biblically speaking. However, many have taken Paul's words "…He also had descended into the lower parts of the earth" (v. 9) as a portrayal of Jesus journeying to Hell during the time between his death and resurrection. Is this what the apostle has in view? Given the use of this phraseology in the Old Testament, it is difficult to argue that Paul was writing about Jesus descending into Hell, much less during his time in the grave. The text contains no reference to the time of Jesus' death – only to his descent from and return to Heaven. Furthermore, there are much more plausible and biblically harmonious explanations. A review of Ephesians 4: 9 will help illuminate Paul's claim.

> Now this *expression*, "He ascended," what does it mean except that He also had descended into the lower parts of the earth? (v. 9)

In this verse, *ascending* and *descending* are joined at the hip. In other words, Jesus' descent to earth is presumed since it serves as an explanation of his presence on earth. Paul is making an argument of logic he believes to be obvious. His point is that for Jesus to ascend to his abode in Heaven, he first descended from Heaven to earth, not from earth to Hell. The claim that Jesus must have descended into Hell in order to be able to ascend to Heaven does not fit with the apostle's reasoning.

Paul's words give a clear impression that Jesus' ascent to Heaven presupposes his earlier descent *to earth*. This meaning seems obvious, but the wording might hold even deeper implications about the descent of which the apostle wrote. It was noted in the twelfth chapter that in Psalm 139: 15 the expression "depths of the earth" is used as a direct reference to a mother's womb (see page 83).

Paul would have been fully cognizant of David's used of this terminology in the Psalm text, so it is reasonable to believe that he might apply that same meaning when writing to the Ephesians about Jesus' descent. In other words, Paul not only recognized *that* Christ descended to earth prior to his ascension, but also offered an allusion to the *manner* of his descent. In all humility, he came into the world (descended to earth) as a baby through the human birthing process. *The Expositor's Bible Commentary* and *The New Bible Commentary*, respectively, offer support for this view:

> **...Paul not only recognized *that* Christ descended to earth prior to his ascension, but also offered an allusion to the *manner* of his descent.**

> Ascension presupposes a prior descent, and Paul describes this as being made into "the lower, earthly regions." The rendering of the NIV takes *ta katotera mere tes ges* (literally, "the lower parts of the earth," RSV) as referring to the incarnation of our Lord.[45]

> The phrase 'the lowest parts of the earth' is probably rightly interpreted by the NIV and GNB, and especially the REB to mean 'the lowest level (of the universe; as seen from heaven)...the point being that the one who ascended and now fills the world...is none other than the one who first descended in humility to incarnation..."[46]

---

[45] Boice, James Montgomery and Wood, Skevington A, *The Expositor's Bible Commentary with the New International Version: Galatians . Ephesians*, Zondervan Publishing House, Grand Rapids, 1995, p 159

[46] Wenham, G. J., Motyer, J. A., Carson, D. A., France, R. T., editors, *New Bible Commentary*, Intervarsity Press, Nottingham, England, 1994, p. 1237

The apostle's rationale in this passage is that Jesus' ascension presumed an earlier descent...but to what did he descend? The only reasonable answer is that Paul has in view Jesus' journey from Heaven to earth. This is the one act that was necessary in order for him to later ascend to Heaven.

Chapter 20
Revelation 1:17-18

The Keys of Death and of Hádes

The Apostle John, in his apocalyptic vision, offers some words concerning the unseen world. In the first chapter, he shares the following thoughts that are spoken by the Messiah.

> ¹⁷ ... I am the first and the last, ¹⁸and I was dead, and behold, I am alive forevermore, and I have the keys of death and of Hades. (Revelation 1: 17b-18)

Jesus, according to John, possesses "the keys of death and of Hádes." This should come as no surprise. Jesus is the ultimate judge who will make the final determination concerning the eternal fortune of every human being. It stands to reason that he should be the one who holds the keys to death and the unseen spiritual domain known as Hádes.

The phrase "the keys of death and of Hádes" should not be understood in earthly terms, but in spiritual terms. The keys represent Christ's *authority* over death and Hádes and not something he might require in order to unlock a door. As God, Jesus has always held this authority in his hands as demonstrated by those whom he raised from the dead as he walked the earth (e.g., Lazarus). Authority over death has always been in God's hands. For this reason, Satan was not allowed to kill Job as he tested him (Job 2: 6). He could only do what God allowed him to do where Job was concerned. It is true that he took the lives of Job's loved ones, which God allowed, but Satan's actions were limited by God's prerogative.

A Battle for the Keys

A specific doctrinal philosophy has been built upon this verse as some have taken considerable liberty with Jesus' words, insisting that the only way he could have the keys of death and Hádes would be by traveling there (after his death and prior to his resurrection) to take the keys. The idea behind this is that, in this verse, death and Hádes are not just spatial realms, but that John's intent was to personify them as spiritual entities rather than spiritual places.

The philosophy that has developed is that, if John intended to personify death and Hádes, then they must be seen, in that personified state, as enemies of Christ. The claim is that for Christ to possess these keys, he *must have* fought a battle with death and Hádes during his days in the tomb – this being the only means available for him to take possession. This stretches the fabric of biblical instruction concerning Jesus' death and resurrection beyond acceptable limits for a number of reasons.

Scripture is clear that Jesus *triumphed* over death. Paul recognizes this in his first letter to the Corinthians as he quoted the Old Testament proclamation, "DEATH HAS BEEN SWALLOWED UP in victory" WHERE, O DEATH, IS YOUR VICTORY? WHERE, O DEATH, IS YOUR STING?" (1 Corinthians 15: 54b-55). With these words, Paul has drawn upon the words of the prophet (Hosea 13: 14). However, according to Paul, Jesus conquered death specifically *through his resurrection*. That is the context in which he cites Hosea. He offered Timothy this same message, writing, "…but has now been revealed by the appearing of our Savior Christ Jesus, who abolished death and brought life and immortality to light through the gospel" (2 Timothy 1: 10). Death was destroyed via the gospel message, which is the death, and particularly the resurrection, of Christ.

Power of Death

Some may wonder about a curious statement by the author of the book of Hebrews suggesting that Satan, at some point in time and in some fashion, held the power of death. According to the writer:

> Therefore, since the children share in flesh and blood, He Himself likewise also partook of the same, so that through death He might destroy the one who has the power of death, that is, the devil. (Hebrews 2: 14)

It is tempting to read more into this verse than the words have to offer. Many turn to the Hebrews text to demonstrate Satan's *power of death*, suggesting that, with these words, he is portrayed as holding the keys of death (and Hádes). This allows them to speculate concerning the spiritual battle during Jesus' days in the tomb where he retrieved the keys from death and Hádes, who had evidently received those keys from Satan.

It is one thing for this author to portray Satan having *the power of death* (Gr. *to kratos echonta tou thanatou*). It would be a completely different matter if he had written that Satan had *power over death* or *authority over death*. These would indicate a measure of control that *power of death* does not. To this can be added the fact that Satan leads people down paths, or lifestyles (drug abuse, etc.), that often lead to premature death among humanity.

The wording here is best understood in abstract terms since the devil was not literally destroyed when Jesus died and rose from the grave. Indeed, he remains to this day. If the wording is not literal, it must be considered figurative. The idea is similar to that in the Timothy passage (above) where Paul wrote that Jesus "abolished death" (2 Timothy 1: 10).

What appears to be in view in the Hebrews passage is the fact that it was Satan who introduced death (both physical and spiritual) into the world of man. In that sense, the very fact of death's existence was on his shoulders. In other words, the devil *owned* (was responsible for) the *power* (consequences) of death. It is the penalty for sin that death represents that is in view in the text. This is how the expression *power of death* is depicted elsewhere in the New Testament (cf. Romans 8: 11). Jesus' resurrection destroyed the effects of the one thing the devil could cite as his unsavory contribution to mankind. This meaning is recognized by Barnes and Coffman, while Jamieson, Fausset, and Brown suggest that it was the very *power of death* that was destroyed, rendering powerless the one who brought death into this world. Consider the following insights.

> I understand this as meaning that the devil was the cause of death in this world. He was the means of its introduction, and of its long and melancholy reign. This does not "affirm" anything of his power of inflicting death in particular instances - whatever may be true on that point - but that "death"

was a part of his dominion; that he introduced it; that he seduced man from God, and led on the train of woes which result in death.[47]

That Satan had the power of death means that, by tempting Adam and Eve to sin and causing them to fall, he was the means of bringing death upon all mankind; and this may be the reason that Satan is called a "murderer" from the beginning (John 8:44).[48]

destroy — literally, "render powerless"; deprive of all power to hurt His people. "That thou mightest still the enemy and avenger" (Psalm 8:2). The same *Greek* verb is used in 2 Timothy 1:10, "abolished death." There is no more death for believers. Christ plants in them an undying seed, the germ of heavenly immortality, though believers have to pass through natural death.

power — Satan is "strong" (Matthew 12:29).

of death — implying that *death* itself is a *power* which, though originally foreign to human nature, now reigns over it (Romans 5:12; Romans 6:9). The power which death has Satan wields. The author of sin is the author of its consequences. [49]

A surprising number of scholars allow for the idea of a battle in Jesus' words concerning *the keys*. However, most who concur with that reading of the passage have already accepted the doctrine of *The Descensus*. This is an example of reading Scripture through a tinted lens. Nothing in Revelation 1: 18 or the surrounding text indicates that Jesus had to *take* the keys of death and Hádes, particularly during his days in the tomb.

In this setting, Jesus is taking the time to explain to the Apostle John what he is witnessing in his vision – he is beholding the Messiah. In fact, the wording suggests that Jesus was the *natural* holder of the keys of death and Hádes since he seems to portray this as a matter of identification for the Son of God. Each statement in the text is intended to demonstrate to John the fact that he was face-to-face with Jesus. He first identifies himself as *the first and the last*. He then calls himself *the living one*. Next, he explains that he is the one *who was dead but is now alive forevermore*. Finally, he is the one *who holds the keys of death and*

---

[47] Barnes, Albert, *Albert Barnes' Notes on the Whole Bible*, https://www.studylight.org/commentaries/eng/bnb/hebrews-2.html, accessed February 6, 2021
[48] Coffman, James B., *James Burton Coffman Commentaries: Hebrews*, A.C.U. Press, Abilene, TX, 1984, p. 51.
[49] Jamieson, Faucett, & Brown, *A Commentary on the Old and New Testaments Volume 3: Matthew-Revelation*, Hendrickson Publishers, Peabody, MA, 2008, p. 532.

Hádes. These four statements could apply to only one individual – Jesus.

There is no mention of a battle, nor does Scripture suggest that God the creator ever surrendered these keys (authority) to anyone. He has always had control over death, and it has always been God who decides who will enter Hádes. Insisting that the passage depicts or alludes to a battle in the spiritual world as Jesus descended to Hell during his days in the tomb necessitates approaching the text with that preconceived notion in view.

Chapter 21

Hell, Hádes, & Paradise

Hell and Hádes

One of the primary issues surrounding the doctrine of *The Descensus* is that people often employ the terms Hell and Hádes loosely and interchangeably. This is even true of many Bible scholars who should be well aware of the distinction between the two domains. It is mankind's failure to distinguish between the two that is partly responsible for the questionable introduction of the expression "He descended into Hell" in the Apostles' Creed.

As noted earlier, the terms She'ol and Hádes are seemingly applied variously in Scripture depending on the context. The mixed use of these terms in Scripture has led to assorted opinions concerning this domain. They do not always specify the spiritual domain known as Hádes – a depository for the souls of the condemned – that is depicted in Jesus' story of the rich man and Lazarus. For instance, the following verses from the NASV speak of She'ol while certain other translations (i.e., KJV, NIV) employ the word *grave* in place of She'ol.

> Then all his sons and all his daughters got up to comfort him, but he refused to be comforted. And he said, "Surely I will go down to Sheol in mourning for my son." So his father wept for him. (Genesis 37: 35)

> Will it go down with me to Sheol? Shall we together go down into the dust? (Job 17: 16)

Some have insisted that She'ol/Hádes *always* depicts the Hádes that is featured in the story of the rich man and Lazarus, but the above verses rebut that claim. For instance, it is unlikely that a righteous man like Jacob, who was father to the twelve tribes of Israel, saw himself condemned to the domain of lost souls after his death (Genesis 37: 35). At the time he made this statement, he was mourning the loss of his favorite son and pictured himself dying in his grief. That is why other English translations have used the term *grave* in this verse.

Where Job is concerned, She'ol is again depicted as a grave, or death (Job 17: 16). The spiritual domain for the lost is not in view in this verse. While *qeber* is the Hebrew word that is often used to depict a grave or gravesite, She'ol is frequently employed to portray the sorrow and agony of death with the grave, or the dust of the earth, presented as a symbol of that sorrow. This represents the most common use of this word in the Old Testament.

On the other hand, there are times when She'ol/Hádes unquestionably represents the spiritual domain where the souls of the lost await the day of final judgment. This is true in the story of the rich man and Lazarus as well as the following verses where something spiritual and mysterious – something beyond death – seems to be in view.

> Sheol below is excited about you, to meet you when you come; It stirs the spirits of the dead for you, all the leaders of the earth; It raises all the kings of the nations from their thrones. (Isaiah 14: 9)

> Though they dig into Sheol, From there My hand will take them; And though they ascend to heaven, From there I will bring them down. (Amos 9: 2)

> Then Death and Hades were thrown into the lake of fire. This is the second death, the lake of fire. (Revelation 20: 14)

It is important to distinguish between the biblical uses of these terms. It is also important to recognize that the terms She'ol and Hádes are never used to represent Hell, the spiritual place of final punishment for the unfaithful. Consequently, a statement like, "For You will not leave my soul in Sheol" (Psalm 16: 10) does not suggest that Jesus traversed to Hell after his death on the cross.

An interesting point is that, while *The First Book of Enoch* is considered a primary source for the doctrine of *The Descensus*, that work does not claim that Jesus visited Hell. It states that Jesus descended to Hádes, with the clear meaning that he descended to the *realm* of the dead, not the spiritual *domain* known as Hádes. Failure to recognize that distinction is what has led to much confusion on this topic.

Paradise in Hádes

Given the dual application of She'ol/Hádes in Scripture, some have wondered whether it is reasonable to conclude that Paradise is located within the confines of Hádes when the term is used generally to depict the realm of the dead. Since Paradise resides in the spiritual world and evidently holds the souls of the faithful, it is safe to say that these spirits are part of that realm. However, it seems wise to draw a distinction between a spiritual realm (i.e., the realm of the dead) and a spiritual domain. Paradise cannot be within the *spiritual domain* known as Hádes when the term represents the domain for lost souls since, according to the Apostle John, after the final judgment, "Then death and Hades were thrown into the lake of fire. The lake of fire is the second death" (Revelation 20: 14). If all who are in Hádes are cast into the fire, Paradise cannot be located there.

If She'ol/Hádes is used as a general term to describe the vastness of the realm of the dead, Paradise seems to fit that category. However, there may be more to the story of Paradise. Many believe that, while Paradise is biblically portrayed as part of the world of the dead (the abode of the souls of the faithful), other texts suggests that it is (now) a part of Heaven – the world of the living – a place of everlasting life. This is based on the *Paradisean Theory*.

The Paradisean Theory

For those well-studied individuals who may be wondering why they have never heard the term *Paradisean Theory*, this is evidently the first time these words have been joined. Consider this the initial introduction of this label making you, as a reader, among the first to see this expression used. The idea itself has existed for many centuries, and a host of Bible scholars subscribe to this theory but, so far as is known, it has never been named. However, the proposed title fits as will be seen over the coming paragraphs.

Identifying and defining Paradise precisely is trickier than one might expect. A question that often arises is whether Abraham's arms and Paradise are one. In Jesus' story about Lazarus and the rich man (Luke 16: 19-31), upon Lazarus's death, Jesus did not say that he went to Paradise, but that he "…was carried away by the angels to Abraham's arms;" (Luke 16: 22). Yet, Jesus promised the thief on the cross, "Truly I say to you, today you shall be with Me in Paradise" (Luke 23: 43).

Does the expression *Abraham's arms* (a.k.a. *Abraham's side* (NIV) or *Abraham's bosom* (KJV)) represent Paradise? If a direct line can be drawn between the story of Lazarus and Jesus' exchange with the thief on the cross, equating Paradise and Abraham's arms seems reasonable. The impression from the narrative is that Lazarus landed in a place identified as Abraham's arms as a blessing in response to the challenges he faced while on earth. Similarly, Jesus' words suggest that the thief would be going with him to a place of comparable blessing after his death.

Biblical teaching on the topic strongly suggests, and most Bible scholars agree, that Paradise and Abraham's arms are one. Therefore, this will be the assumption going forward. The challenge that arises is explaining why a place identified as Paradise, which Scripture indicates is either Heaven or a part of Heaven, would be so accessible, both visually and vocally, from Hádes. The two (Hádes and Abraham's arms) are described as being separated by a "great chasm" (Luke 16: 26), yet the rich man could, at least in an allegorical sense, both see and converse with Abraham. If Paradise is Heaven or a component of Heaven, it is puzzling to see how or why those in Hádes might be allowed to communicate with anyone in Heaven (Paradise) in any way. The answer to this mystery may lie in what has been termed here, the *Paradisean Theory*.

Given the biblical depiction of Paradise, it could be argued that it served as a place of waiting for those faithful who died prior to Christ's death and resurrection and, when Jesus ascended, those who had been waiting were transported to Heaven as Paradise was relocated there. Some believe this is the meaning of certain verses like the following one written by the Apostle Paul.

[7] But to each one of us grace was given according to the measure of Christ's gift. [8] Therefore it says,

"WHEN HE ASCENDED ON HIGH,
HE LED CAPTIVE *THE* CAPTIVES,
AND HE GAVE GIFTS TO PEOPLE." (Ephesians 4: 7-8)

Paul is citing Psalms 68: 18. The idea, it is said, is that when Jesus ascended to Heaven after his death, he took with him the faithful who had previously passed from this life who had been waiting in Paradise. It could be argued that this was the moment dramatic changes occurred in the spirit world and, after Jesus' ascension, the faithful would no longer be sent to the realm of the dead as Paradise was removed to Heaven. Coffman says of Paul's statement:

> There is an obvious allusion here to one of Paul's favorite comparisons, that of the conquering Christ leading the type of triumphal parade affected by Roman emperors.[50]

Paul, writing about Jesus' ascension, pictures him leading a parade reminiscent of victorious Roman emperors. Whether Paul has in view Jesus triumphantly leading those who had been waiting in Paradise is difficult to say. In fairness, that may not be the point Coffman is attempting to make, but some believe this to be the case. It would help explain why, in the Lazarus/rich man narrative, Paradise is portrayed in proximity to Hádes, but is later depicted by both Paul and John as a heavenly domain.

No real consensus is found among the Apostolic and Early Church Fathers as they penned assorted views concerning Paradise in the centuries following Jesus' ascension. Papias (AD 60-130), one of the Apostolic Fathers of the early church, sought to *classify* heavenly domains based on who would dwell in each as a measure of their heavenly reward, saying of Paradise, "…the second class will dwell in Paradise."[51] This is a view that was shared by Irenaeus (AD 130-202). Origen (AD 185-254), on the other hand, apparently saw Paradise as a terranean setting reserved for the faithful, stating, "I think, therefore, that all the saints who depart from this life will remain in some place situated on the earth, which holy Scripture calls paradise."[52] Others like Tertullian (AD 160-220) and Cyprian (AD 200-258) evidently believed that Paradise serves as a temporary haven of rest beyond death prior to the Second Coming, but only for Christian martyrs. Consequently, no

---

[50] Coffman, James B., *James Burton Coffman Commentaries: Galatians, Ephesians, Philippians, Colossians*, U.C.U. Press, Abiline, TX, 1977, p. 186
[51] Papias, *The Kingdom in the Early Church Fathers* (godskingdomfirst.org), accessed February 10, 2021.
[52] Origen, *First Principles, Book II, CHAP XI.6, The Kingdom in the Early Church Fathers (godskingdomfirst.org)*, accessed February 10, 2021.

solid information about Paradise can be drawn from the writings of the early church.

While the *Paradisean Theory* is not scripturally *provable* (it is only a theory), it does complement and help to explain parts of the biblical narrative as certain verses seem to offer a measure of support. It serves to explain the rich man's partial access to Paradise prior to the ascension (Luke 16: 22-23) even as Paul and John later portray Paradise as a heavenly domain (2 Corinthians 12: 2-4; Revelation 2: 7).

Chapter 22

Peering Behind the Stone

Reasoned Inference

This chapter is more contemplative than conclusive. The truth is, little is known, biblically speaking, about Jesus' time in the spiritual world prior to his resurrection. Still, Scripture offers certain statements that can provide some guidance for that period of time. Beyond these few remarks, most claims about Jesus' time in the tomb are derived inferentially. Therefore, this chapter could aptly be titled *Reasoned Inference About Jesus' Time in the Tomb*.

With that in mind, no one should take what is written here as Holy Spirit-inspired revelation or incontrovertible biblical interpretation. Scripture offers little information about Jesus' days in the tomb. This chapter contains assorted views and possibilities concerning Jesus' time in the tomb based on exceedingly sparse biblical details.

Hádes vs. Hell

Although there are assorted views when it comes to some of the details, there is one eschatological matter where everyone seems to be in relative agreement. There is a biblically-based consensus in Christendom that there will be a time of final judgment (Revelation 6: 10; 14: 7) – often referred to as *the day of the Lord* (cf. Hebrews 10: 25; 2 Peter 3: 10). This is important since it speaks to the role of Hell (the lake of fire) in eschatology. According to the Apostle John, at the final judgment:

And the beast was seized, and with him the false prophet who performed the signs in his presence, by which he deceived those who had received the mark of the beast and those who worshiped his image; these two were thrown alive into the **lake of fire**, which burns with brimstone. (Revelation 19: 20) Emphasis added

[10]…the devil who deceived them was thrown into the **lake of fire** and brimstone, where the beast and the false prophet *are* also; and they will be tormented day and night forever and ever… [14] Then Death and Hades were thrown into the **lake of fire**. This is the second death, the **lake of fire**. [15] And if anyone's name was not found written in the book of life, he was thrown into the **lake of fire**. (Revelation 20: 10, 14-15) Emphasis added

There is no indication in the pages of Scripture that anyone has yet descended to Hell, even in the twenty first century. It is depicted as the domain of final punishment for the unfaithful following the final judgment. Hádes is not Hell. Tartarus/the Abyss/the Pit (all seemingly names of a single spiritual domain), do not represent Hell. Besides the verses just cited from Revelation, following are the only verses of Scripture where Hell (Gehenna) is mentioned.

[22] But I say to you that everyone who is angry with his brother shall be answerable to the court; and whoever says to his brother, 'You good-for-nothing,' shall be answerable to the supreme court; and whoever says, 'You fool,' shall be guilty *enough to go* into the fiery **Hell**. [29] Now if your right eye is causing you to sin, tear it out and throw it away from you; for it is better for you to lose one of the parts of your *body*, than for your whole body to be thrown into **Hell**. [30] And if your right hand is causing you to sin, cut it off and throw it away from you; for it is better for you to lose one of the parts of your *body*, than for your whole body to go into **Hell**. (Matthew 5: 22, 29-30) Emphasis added

And do not be afraid of those who kill the body but are unable to kill the soul; but rather fear Him who is able to destroy both soul and body in **Hell**. (Matthew 10: 28) Emphasis added

And if your eye is causing you to sin, tear it out and throw it away from you. It is better for you to enter life with one eye, than to have two eyes and be thrown into the fiery **Hell**. (Matthew 18: 9) Emphasis added

"Woe to you, scribes and Pharisees, hypocrites, because you travel around on sea and land to make one proselyte; and when he becomes *one*, you make him twice as much a son of **Hell** as yourselves. (Matthew 23: 15) Emphasis added

⁴³And if your hand causes you to sin, cut it off; it is better for you to enter life maimed, than, having your two hands, to go into **Hell**, into the unquenchable fire… ⁴⁵And if your foot is causing you to sin, cut it off; it is better for you to enter life without a foot, than, having your two feet, to be thrown into **Hell**… ⁴⁷And if your eye is causing you to sin, throw it away; it is better for you to enter the kingdom of God with one eye, than, having two eyes, to be thrown into **Hell** (Mark 9: 43, 45, 47) Emphasis added

And the tongue is a fire, the *very* world of unrighteousness; the tongue is set among our body's parts as that which defiles the whole body and sets on fire the course of *our* life, and is set on fire by **Hell**. (James 3: 6) Emphasis added

Certain other passages serve up an allusion to Hell (generally with the term *fire*) as a place of punishment, although they do not use the term Hell. These are mostly limited to the gospels and Revelation, and include (Matthew 3: 10-12; 7: 19; 13: 40, 42, 50; 18: 8; 25: 41; Mark 9: 43, 48-49; Luke 3: 9, 17; John 15: 6; Hebrews 10: 26; James 5: 3; 2 Peter 3: 7; Jude 1: 7; Revelation 14: 10; 15: 2; 16: 8; 17: 16; 18: 8; 19: 20; 21: 8).

The above passages are the only verses in both the Old and New Testaments where Hell is mentioned, and they all offer warnings about future punishment. Not one of these verses depicts Jesus visiting that particular spiritual domain. Notice also that none of these uses of the word Hell (or fire) is directly or indirectly linked with Jesus' time in the tomb.

Jesus in Hádes

Certain verses of Scripture, when viewed through a specific theological lens, seem to suggest that Jesus may have been in Hádes and/or the Abyss after his death, so these texts must be given consideration. Arguably, the most famous passages that lend themselves to this point of view are those that were discussed in chapters eleven and seventeen (Psalm 16: 10; Acts 2: 27) where the verse in Acts is simply a reciting of the verse from the Psalms.

¹⁰ For You will not abandon my soul to Sheol;
You will not allow Your Holy One to undergo decay (Psalm 16: 10)

²⁷ FOR YOU WILL NOT ABANDON MY SOUL TO HADES,
NOR WILL YOU ALLOW YOUR HOLY ONE TO UNDERGO DECAY.
(Acts 2: 27)

As discussed in those earlier chapters, these verses seem to depict She'ol/Hádes as the tomb – a place where Jesus' body could see decay – rather than a spiritual realm. However, it is also true that these terms are used to portray the realm of the dead generally. Consequently, it is arguable that these verses may have a dual meaning.

Jesus died a physical death comparable to the death that has been, or will be, experienced by every human being, save those for whom special provision has been made or those who remain alive at the Second Coming. That means his death involved the separation of his body and spirit at which time his spirit would have journeyed to the realm of the dead (She'ol/Hádes) rather than Hell. Therefore, a dual meaning is not out of the question.

Jesus Went to Paradise

One of the thieves who was crucified next to Jesus humbled himself before the Lord and simply asked that Jesus would remember him. The thief's request, with the words, "…when You come in Your kingdom!" (Luke 23: 42), appears to suggest that he may have been looking to a future time when Jesus might remember him. Jesus' response indicates that the man's request would be answered swiftly. He would be with Jesus in Paradise that very day (Luke 23: 43).

Because the Greek fails to include punctuation marks, some have taken considerable liberty with Jesus' words to the thief – particularly those who believe in *soul sleep*, which was discussed early in the book. Insisting that spiritual rewards will only be delivered upon Jesus' Second Coming, some have chosen to reconfigure the verse, claiming that, while Jesus may have made the promise as the two hung on their respective crosses, that promise could not be fulfilled immediately. In that vein, the English syntax has been adjusted accordingly, with the verbiage; *Truly I say to you today, you shall be with Me in Paradise.* Placing the comma after "today" suggests that Jesus was identifying the time the promise was given and not the time of its fulfillment.

The fact is that no English Bible translation, whether literal, paraphrased, or common, has recognized this as a legitimate rendering of Jesus' words. Barnes effectively addressed this curious effort to glean from Jesus' words something he did not say.

> **To-day shalt thou be with me in …** it is no wonder that those who have embraced the contrary opinion should endeavor to explain away this

meaning. In order to do this, a comma is placed after σημερον, to-day, and then our Lord is supposed to have meant, "Thou shalt be with me after the resurrection I tell thee this, To-Day." I am sorry to find men of great learning and abilities attempting to support this most feeble and worthless criticism. Such support a good cause cannot need; and, in my opinion, even a bad cause must be discredited by it.[53]

The timing of the fulfillment of Jesus' promise to the thief is significant in that it addresses the period immediately following Jesus' death. Where Jesus' statement to the thief is concerned, no inference is required to understand his words. Upon their deaths (today), the two would cross over to the spiritual domain known as Paradise, offering students of Scripture a measure of insight into at least one facet of Jesus' spiritual activity after his crucifixion and prior to his resurrection on the first day of the week.

Jesus in Paradise

Jesus told the thief that they would be heading to Paradise when they both passed from this earth. That is an unequivocal statement straight from Jesus' lips and explains where Jesus' spirit went as his body lay in the tomb. He joined with the faithful in Paradise. Any other claim is purely extrabiblical speculation and has no scriptural footing. One might ask, then: *What happened when Jesus arrived in Paradise?*

According to the narrative, when Lazarus was resting in Abraham's arms (Paradise), this domain was at least semi-accessible from Hádes. Lazarus could not cross over to Hádes, nor could the rich man cross over to Abraham's arms, but there was, at least in the parabolic situation that is given, an element of communication between them. Yet, at that time, no hint is given that Paradise and Heaven were one. It is only later, in Paul's second letter to the Corinthians, that Paradise is described as Heaven, or a component of Heaven (2 Corinthians 12: 4). The Apostle John recognized a similar connection (Revelation 2: 7).

Is it possible that Jesus visited spiritual domains other than Paradise prior to his resurrection on the third day? It is possible, but nothing in God's Word leads to that conclusion. It is also possible, given the story of Lazarus, that Jesus could have communicated with those in the domain of Hádes as he visited Paradise. Could this be the meaning behind Peter's

---

[53] Barnes, Albert, *Albert Barnes' Notes on the Whole Bible*, https://wwww.studylight.org/commentaries/bnb/luke-23.html, accessed September 19, 2020.

words about Jesus *proclaiming to spirits in prison* (1 Peter 3: 19)? That seems unlikely for two reasons. First, that proclamation was either directly aimed at, or specifically impacted, Noah's contemporaries rather than the countless multitudes awaiting judgment in Hádes (1 Peter 3: 20). Second, as Dalton explained in his book *Christ's Proclamation to the Spirits – A Study of 1 Peter 3:18-4:6*, the apostle's narrative indicates that Jesus' proclamation occurred after the resurrection (1 Peter 3: 18-19).

Conclusion

Did Jesus descend into Hell (Gehenna)? It is a question that has perplexed scholars and laymen alike over the past two millennia. People on each side of the debate are not only confident in their position on the subject, but they are also sincerely passionate where this topic is concerned, despite the fact that it is completely unrelated to one's salvation. With that in mind, here are some factual statements concerning Scripture and *The Descensus*:

1. The only clear statement contained in God's Word about Jesus' time in the spiritual world after his death are his words to the thief on the cross. At that time, Jesus plainly stated that the thief would be joining him in Paradise *that day* (Luke 43: 23).

2. No verse of Scripture speaks overtly to Jesus descending into Hell. Of those passages that specifically mention Hell, not one depicts Jesus visiting this loathsome spiritual domain.

3. When hermeneutical principles are properly applied, there is no biblical/exegetical reason to insist that the Hebrew *u·m·themuth e·artz* (cf. Isaiah 44: 23) or the Greek *katōtera merē tēs gēs,* translated *the lower parts of the earth* (cf. Ephesians 4: 9), is intended to reference Hell.

4. Scripture provides no teaching about souls being introduced to Hell (Gehenna) prior to the final judgment (Revelation 20: 15). Hence, had Jesus journeyed there after his death, it appears that he would have been greeted by an empty domain.

The doctrine of *The Descensus* relies far more on extra-biblical literature than on Scripture. Those Bible passages that are used to depict Jesus' descent are often *explained* through secular texts and oral tradition. To this can be added the fact that no verse of Scripture, unaided by awkward analytics and questionable inference, portrays Jesus descending to the spiritual domain known as Hell.

It is an irrefutable biblical truth that, accompanied by the thief who died on the cross next to him, Jesus' spirit journeyed to Paradise after his death (Luke 23: 43). There he undoubtedly visited with the souls of the saved, perhaps even preparing them for their transition to Heaven if the *Paradisean Theory* can be believed. However, when it comes to the claim that Jesus descended to Hell, it seems this is a doctrine born, not of Scripture nor of the apostles, but of the imaginative minds of men.

Bibliography

https://www.biblestudytools.com/dictionary/Gehenna/,

St., Augustine, CHURCH FATHERS: Letter 164 (St. Augustine) (newadvent.org),

St., Augustine, Letter clxiv. (A. D. 414). https://biblehub.com/library/augustine/the_confessions_and_letters_of_st/letter_clxiv_a_d_414.htm.

Barnes, Albert, *Albert Barnes' Notes on the Whole Bible*, https://www.studylight.org/commentaries/bnb/psalms-16.html.

Barnes, Albert, *Albert Barnes' Notes on the Whole Bible*, https://www.studylight.org/commentaries/bnb/psalms-88.html.

Barnes, Albert, *Albert Barnes' Notes on the Whole Bible*, https://wwww.studylight.org/commentaries/bnb/luke-23.html

Barnes, Albert, *Albert Barnes' Notes on the Whole Bible*, https://www.studylight.org/ commentaries/eng/bnb/romans-10.html.

Barnes, Albert, *Albert Barnes' Notes on the Whole Bible*, https://www.studylight.org/commentaries/eng/bnb/hebrews-2.html

Boice, James Montgomery and Wood, Skevington A, *The Expositor's Bible Commentary with the New International Version: Galatians . Ephesians,* Zondervan Publishing House, Grand Rapids, 1995

Bruce, F. F., General Editor, *The New International Bible Commentary*, Zondervan, Grand Rapids, 1979

The Cambridge Bible for Schools and Colleges https://biblehub.com/ commentaries/ cambridge/1_peter/4.htm

Carlson, Steven A., *One Bible...And Yet, So Many Beliefs*, Guardian Publishing, LLC, Holt, MI, 2014

Clark, Adam, *Clarke's Commentary Volume II: Joshua-Esther*, Abingdon-Cokesbury Press. New York-Nashville

Clarke, Adam, *Clarke's Commentary Volume III: Book of Job-Song of Solomon*, Abingdon-Cokesbury Press, New York-Nashville

Coffman, James B., *James Burton Coffman's Commentaries on the Bible*, https://studylight.org/commentaries/bcc/Ezekiel-26.html

Coffman, James B., *James Burton Coffman Commentaries: Romans*, A.C.U. Press, Houston, TX, 1973

Coffman, James B., *James Burton Coffman Commentaries: Galatians, Ephesians, Philippians, Colossians*, U.C.U. Press, Abilene, TX, 1977, p. 186

Coffman, James B., *James Burton Coffman Commentaries: Hebrews*, A.C.U. Press, Abilene, TX, 1984

Coffman, J. B., *James Burton Coffman Commentaries: James 1 & 2 Peter, 1, 2 & 3 John, Jude*, A. C. U. Press, Abilene, TX, 1984.

Coffman, James B., Coffman's Commentaries on the Bible, https://www.studylight.org/commentaries/bcc/ezekiel-26.html.

Dalton, William, *Christ's Proclamation to the Spirits – A Study of 1 Peter 3:18-4:6*, Catholic Theological College, Melbourne, 1989

Ellicott, Charles J., *Ellicott's Commentary for English Readers*, https://www.studylight.org/commentaries/ebc/psalms-16 html.

Ericson, Norman R., *Spirits in Prison*, https://www.biblestudytools.com/dictionaries/bakers-evangelical-dictionary/spirits-in-prison.html.

Expositor's Bible Commentary, https://biblehub.com/commentaries/expositors/1_peter/4.htm.

Holdcroft, Mark, *Baptism*, https://www.sermoncentral.com/sermons/baptism-mark-holdcroft-sermon-on-baptism-59607.

Jamieson, Faucett, & Brown, *A Commentary on the Old and New Testaments Volume 1: Genesis-Esther*, Hendrickson Publishers, Peabody, MA, 2008

Jamieson, Faucett, & Brown, *A Commentary on the Old and New Testaments Volume 2: Job-Malachi*, Hendrickson Publishers, Peabody, MA, 2008

Jamieson, Faucett, & Brown, *A Commentary on the Old and New Testaments Volume 3: Matthew-Revelation*, Hendrickson Publishers, Peabody, MA, 2008

Jensen, Richard, *Commentary on 1 Peter 1: 3-9*, http://www.workingpreacher.org/preaching.aspx?commentary_id=57.

Kelly, William, *William Kelly Major Works Commentary*, https://biblehub.com/commentaries/kelly/1_peter/4.htm.

MacLaren, Alexander, https://biblehub.com/commentaries/maclaren/1_peter/4.htm.

Marshall, Taylor, Descended into Hell – Latin and Greek Versions of the Apostles' Creed, *Descended into Hell - Latin and Greek versions of Apostles Creed - Taylor Marshall*

McGarvey, J. W. and Pendleton, Philip Y., *A Commentary on Thessalonians, Corinthians, Galatians, and Romans*, Gospel Light Publishing, Delight, AR, p. 158.

Meyer, Frederick B., https://biblehub.com/commentaries/meyer/1_peter/4.htm,

Origen, *First Principles*, Book II, CHAP XI.6, The Kingdom in the Early Church Fathers (godskingdomfirst.org)

Piper, John, *Does My Soul Sleep After Death?* https://www.desiringgod.org/interviews/does-my-soul-sleep-after-death.

The Pulpit Commentary, https://biblehub.com/commentaries/pulpit/1_peter/4.htm

Rufinus, Tyrannius, Commentary on the Apostles' Creed, *CHURCH FATHERS: Commentary on the Apostles' Creed (Rufinus) (newadvent.org)*

Slick, Matt, *Jesus' Resurrection was Physical*, Christian Apologetics and Research Ministry, https://carm.org/jesus-resurrection-was-physical.

Wenham, G. J., Motyer, J. A., Carson, D. A., France, R. T., editors, New Bible Commentary, Intervarsity Press, Nottingham, England, 1994,

www.ingramcontent.com/pod-product-compliance
Lightning Source LLC
Chambersburg PA
CBHW051807040426
42446CB00007B/555